ASPECTS OF BRADFORD

ASPECTS *of* BRADFORD

Discovering Local History

Edited by
Bob Duckett

Series Editor
Brian Elliott

Wharncliffe Publishing

First Published in 1999 by
Wharncliffe Publishing
an imprint of
Pen and Sword Books Limited,
47 Church Street, Barnsley,
South Yorkshire. S70 2AS

Copyright © Wharncliffe Publishing 1999

For up-to-date information on other titles produced under the
Wharncliffe imprint, please telephone or write to:

> **Wharncliffe Publishing**
> **FREEPOST**
> **47 Church Street**
> **Barnsley**
> **South Yorkshire S70 2BR**
> **Telephone (24 hours): 01226 - 734555**

ISBN: 1-871647-55-X

A CIP catalogue record of this book is available from the
British Library

Cover illustration: Broadstones, Bradford. Water colour by N.C. Crichton, 1853-1913.
Bradford Arts, Museums and Library Service.

Printed in Great Britain by
Redwood Books, Trowbridge, Wiltshire

CONTENTS

INTRODUCTION

by Bob Duckett

As I leave home for work in the mornings, I leave my modern house that once was not there. I remember it not being there. On their way to school years ago, my children used to feed the horses that grazed in the field in which our home would later be built. As I enter the road noisy with rush hour traffic, I pass a massive dressed stone gatepost, leading nowhere. Old maps tell me it once marked the entrance to the stately tree-lined drive of a large house. The drive and house are now gone, buried beneath a busy road and 1970s semis. Only a gatepost remains, and a dwindling number of old trees; though the historically literate will recognise the name of the family who lived in the house in the name of the road.

Across the road I see a tree-lined snicket. Now used only by dog-walkers, families on Sunday afternoons, and children seeking conkers in the autumn, it was, before the days of asphalt and cars, a busy thoroughfare. The drystone walls are still magnificant. It was once called Slaughter Lane on account, so the history books tell me, of some killings when Jacobins from Scotland raided this far south.

Across the valley I see a canal, a train, a radio aerial, housing estates and factories, all with stories to tell. And on the moors, away from the boggy valley bottoms, are older tracks, some still with stone slabs - causeys - which may have seen trains of pack horses, perhaps taking wool from the abbey estates or workers' cottages to market. And Roman roads, perhaps witness to a cohort of soldiers en route to Mancunium from the legionary headquarters at Eboriacum (York), having stopped overnight at Olicana (Ilkley). And even older tracks, waymarked by standing stones, some with carvings. And what of the giant Rombald himself, after whom the moor is named? What happened here all those years ago?

The more we are conscious of the past, the more we value what remains, whether it be physical – a building or landmark; memories – ours, and those of others; and documents such as photographs, maps, archives, and books. And then we realize how important it is to preserve and record the present, for without our memories and memorials, we would have no past! Even if we remember, what of those to come? What will be their view of us? It is for this reason I am pleased to add this volume on Bradford to the *Aspects* series of books on local history.

Saltaire Village and Salts Mill may seem permanent enough, but without the dedication and vision of its residents and entrepreneurs, it would not be the thriving community it is today. I thank bookseller Clive Woods, a major player himself, for chronicling the story.

I have always admired the marvellous buildings of Keighley, but they mean so much more now that John Waddington-Feather, Keighley born and bred, and proud of it, has told me his memories of them. Beyond the buildings, are those who used them, and many surprises!

Some buildings are mere shells of their former selves. An unusual account by librarian David Croft records the place of fire in Bradford's history. More orthodox in treatment is that by Brontë Birthplace owner, Barbara Whitehead, and her account of Thornton. Less orthodox, though, are the striking photographs she uses to illustrate her account. These were taken by Richard Newman, whose gift for the unusual and atmospheric is given full rein in his own selection of 'favourite haunts and hidden corners'.

However hard we look though, it needs the memories of Frank Long to tell us what it was like to drive trolleybuses and what parcel lads did; and the reminiscences of Alex Robinson to tell us what it was like to work in a pharmacy before the war, before prepackaged and branded 'products'. Those smells! And it needs the memories of Frederick Taglione to describe what it was like to be a member of an immigrant community, Italian in his case, but I'm sure his account will strike chords with members of other immigrant communities.

The lives of two famous Bradfordians are recorded by Philip Colehan and Ronnie Wharton. Philip was a life-long friend of John Braine, author of *Room at the Top*. The account of John's years in Bradford and Bingley, on his way to the Top, makes a fascinating read. Ronnie tells the tragic story of the Broomfields hero, Jerry Delaney, who, but for the Battle of the Somme, could well have become Bradford's first national boxing champion.

A forgotten aspect of the 1914-18 war is Bradford's part in building seaplanes. Museum curator Eugene Nicholson and his colleagues blow dust off hidden blueprints and bring to our notice a little known piece of Bradford history. Finally, although little enough remains of medieval Bradford, the Manor Court Rolls survive, and in Geoffrey Greenhough we are fortunate to have someone to bring the Bradfordians of olden times back to life. And what lives!

And so, through memories and memorials, buildings and books, research and reminiscence, writing and reading, my authors and I present you with *Aspects of Bradford 1*.

I wish to acknowledge the help I have recieved from my colleagues at work, particularly Carol Greenwood, Gina Szekely and Peter Walker, for advice on local history, the English language, and computer discs respectively. Tracey Ambler efficiently keyboarded three typescripts for me, Jan Coleman has provided an excellent index, and for photographs I am indebted to Dorothy Burrows, Stanley King, Mary Tate, Frances Wood, Jackie Kitwood, Pam Booth, Ann Davies, Christine Hopper, Anthea Bickley, Ian Ward and Tim Smith. Good advice was given by Ian Dewhirst and Pauline Barfield, *Aspects* series editor Brian Elliott, and the ever-cheerful Mike Parsons of Wharncliffe Publishing. My thanks to all my contributors, and to those whose contributions I had to leave out. Ever the optimist, they are at the head of the queue for *Aspects of Bradford 2*.

Bob Duckett
Bradford Reference Library
May 1999

Note: Anyone interested in making a contribution to *Aspects of Bradford 2* should, in the first instance, contact Bob Duckett, c/o Wharncliffe Publishing, 47 Church Street, Barnsley, S70 2AS enclosing a brief description of their work.

1. LAW AND DISORDER IN MEDIEVAL BRADFORD

by Geoffrey H Greenhough

A WHOLE MILLENNIUM before Bradford's manorial records began, the Roman legions were in what we now call the central part of Yorkshire. Successful elsewhere, they conspicuously failed in their attempts to subdue the wild tribesmen who eked out an existence on the inhospitable moors of the Pennine foothills. Several centuries after the departure of the Roman occupation forces, the Danes devised a better way: having conquered York (and divided the county into what they called 'thridings', our 'Ridings') they infiltrated the whole area, building their own settlements and giving to them place names that reflected the Danish language of the inhabitants. Their words found their way too into the dialect spoken both east and west of the Pennine range.

The various place-names ending in 'thorpe', a farmstead, remind us that the Danes once lived among the earlier settlers, who called their farmstead a 'wic' (Wyke, to the south of the city, has a Saxon name). Other place names from the Danes include 'garth', 'beck' and 'ing' as in Hall Ings. Danish words that have survived in the local dialect are 'laik' meaning to play, 'skeller' meaning to warp, 'addle' meaning to earn, and 'natter' meaning to worry.

Bradford and its surrounding area succumbed to this infiltration. By the time of the Norman conquest, ownership of land and property was in the hands of the descendants of those Danish settlers. But in the generations following 1066, new overlords were appointed from the ranks of the Norman invaders. The Lacy family had crossed the English Channel and fought alongside William of Normandy and was given Pontefract, holding those vast tracts of land that included the Manor of Bradford. But in 1327, the Lacy family had forfeited their lands to the crown, which settled them on the Duchy of Lancaster.

During the fourteenth century, the manor of Bradford was farmed out to the highest bidder, who then enjoyed the proceeds of tolls from the markets and fairs. Successive tenants built manor houses, and established their feudal rights to hold courts and to control the economic life of the area. Of these major tenants, very little is known. Regarding people of lower social class in the manor of Bradford,

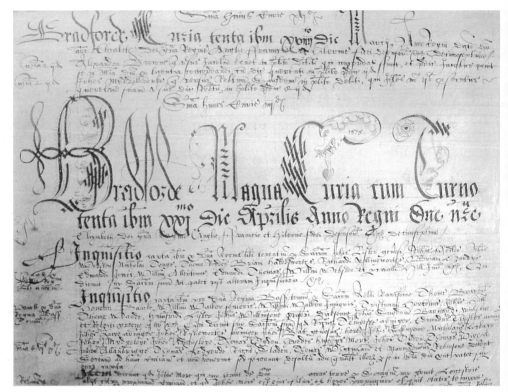

Figure 1. The opening page of one of the original manuscripts of Bradford's Manor Court Rolls. *Bradford Libraries*

practically nothing that may have been recorded of them has survived. There was a peasantry which included both bondsmen and freemen, but in what proportions it was bond or free is a matter of conjecture. Certainly, none of the statistics that relate to social structures in the south of England can be relied on: the Pennine area was geographically separate from the more populous south, and the people scratched a living that must have bordered on acute poverty and deprivation. Statistics that were preserved were generally about wealth and property: the actual residents of Bradford had little of either. Perhaps for that reason, even the Subsidy Rolls, recording the revenue that was collected, have not survived.

The Court Rolls alone record some aspects of life in Bradford. The earliest surviving Rolls begin in 1339, and are of course written in Latin. Those dating up to around 1500 are held in the Public Record Office, later ones are still in private hands. The early Rolls

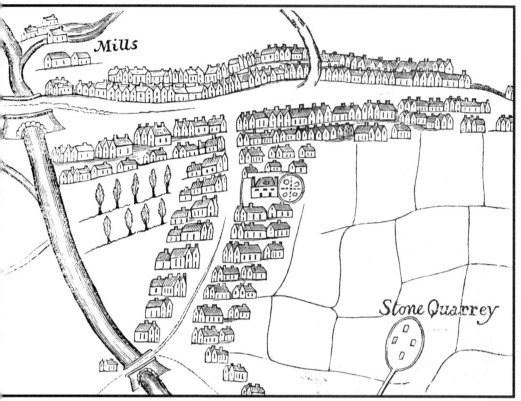

Figure 2. An early map of Bradford from John James' *History and Topography of Bradford*, 1841. *Bradford Libraries*

were translated just before the First World War, and the bound volumes of hand-written foolscap are held in the Bradford Central Library. These volumes are the primary source of information for this chapter.

Life in Bradford for Tenants and Peasants

Inevitably, the court records are concerned with maintaining law and order, and dealing with offenders. Prominent members of the community were called to serve in the Court, and their names are preserved. Landowners appear also, usually in disputes over rights and ownership. But the only peasants who appear are those accused of offences: the law-abiding majority have no mention. In any study of the Court Rolls, one is dealing with a section, and not a representative cross-section, of the community.

Constables for the various vills (townships) are regularly appointed. Their names are recorded, and for generations the names are the same. As son succeeded father, the onus of maintaining order in the tiny communities devolved upon the small, landed, farmers. They also appear as jurymen, and an early list of these, dating from 1354, reads

Robert de Cordonlai
William del Bolling
William del Neuhal
Henry del Neuhal
Adam de Wik
Robert de Roulai.

These names, eventually becoming surnames, appear through the centuries, Cordingley being perhaps one of the most prominent.

Bondsmen and Freemen were numbered among the peasantry,

Figure 3. Bradford at the time of Charles 1st. From a drawing by S.C.Bailey in W.Claridge *Origin and history of the Bradford Grammar School*, 1882. *Bradford Libraries*

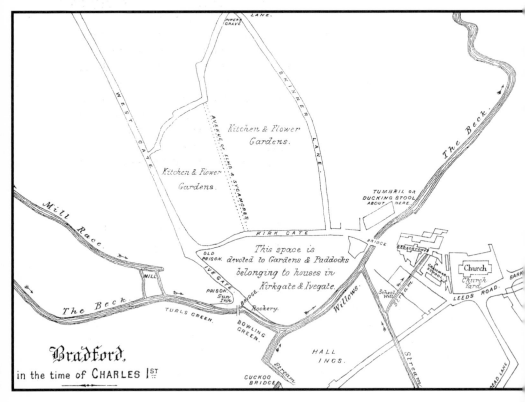

Figure 4. Queen Philippa. Edward III became king in 1327 at 15 years of age, and within six months married the fourteen-year-old Philippa. Edward was reckless with money. His mother, Isabella, had seized Philippa's dowry. Philippa's household lived on occasional grants from the Exchequer until in 1330 permanent provision was made by the grant of Pontefract, its castle and borough, 'with the castles, towns, manors and other appurtenances.' One of these was the Manor of Bradford. There is no record of Philippa ever entering the town, but the Courts were held in her name and the revenues duly paid to her. Philippa had twelve children, the second most prolific queen in our history, and she is a direct ancestor of the House of Windsor.
Mary Evans Picture Library

and the distinction between them was being blurred by this time. But still, a bondsman could not transfer his land, or leave his manor, without permission. In 1354, the status was carefully stated:

'Margery, daughter of Thomas Newcomen, and William Dunker, bondmen of the lord.' The same year, fines were imposed on 'Cecelia de la More a bondwoman deflowered by John Judson'. A married couple were fined for getting married without permission: 'Isabella, daughter of William Childyong a bondwoman ... married to a certain William Cisson a free man, without permission'. Enquiries were made by the Court to forcibly return to the Manor of Bradford 'the sons and daughters of William del Munker who dwell at Darlington [and] are bondmen' and 'Alice daughter of William Childyong a bondwoman of the lord [who] dwells at York'.

Plague
The 'Extent' of 1341, covering Bradford, Manningham, Horton and Stanbury, listed all those who held land, but not sub-tenants. The holdings were classified according to size:

67 holdings were of less than 10 acres
25 were between 10 and 20 acres
23 were stated to be 'at will', i.e. without firm title

None of the holdings were at all large, and this indicates a low level of prosperity. Eight years later, the plague struck Bradford, reducing the population by an estimated 23% and devastating an already precarious economy. Those who survived the plague (this was the last time that the plague occurred) suffered a sharp fall in living standards. Rents for land tumbled, and there was a reduced demand for market stalls.

The Court Rolls for the summer of 1350 tell a sad story of rapid deaths:

> *Alice daughter of John Kyng of Horton ... claimed for herself ... without Joan and Juliana her sisters, after the decease of Robert Kyng kinsman of the said Alice, whose heir she is, one messuage two bovates and a half of land with the appurtenances, in Horton by fealty of service of 6s 6d by the year and one day's work in autumn or one and a half pence and to do suit of the Court in Bradford every three weeks and a duplication of her rent in name [= by way] of relief for all other services. And whereas the tenements aforesaid now in the Pestilence descended to a certain John Kyng her kinsman and afterwards to the aforesaid Robert, and now to the aforesaid Alice without paying relief, now the aforesaid Alice is charge with three reliefs, to wit: 38s 6d.*

All this happened within a year! Eight years later, the Court recognised the son of John Bulle, now of age, to take over 'the fourth part of a bovate of land, with the appurtenances in ... Standbiri'. John had died in the plague. One wonders what state the land was in after nearly nine years of neglect. The same year, 1358, the Court noted that 'one shamble in Bradford lies in the hand of the lord for default of a tenant and has so lain in the lord's hand from the time of the plague until now'.

But a tenant appeared. Before the plague the rent for the shamble had been 4d per annum. Now

> *came John Milner and took the shamble aforesaid ... rendering therefor by the year 8d at the accustomed terms and for which same rent it is granted to the said John Milner and his heirs as long as they shall hold that shamble that they may be quit of toll in Bradford and elsewhere when it is convenient and the aforesaid John gives nothing in fine because (it was) in the lord's hand for default of tenant and it is let at 4d beyond the ancient rent.*

Work

As in so many communities, the people of Bradford suffered greatly because of the changes from tillage to sheep-farming. Overlords dispossessed their agricultural workers all through the fourteenth century in order to profit from the much higher return from sheep, valued for their milk, their wool, their manure and their meat. A sheep-rearing economy necessitated the clearance of smallholdings where peasants provided for their families according to long-established manorial custom. In some cases, though not in Bradford, whole villages were cleared and demolished. Bradford became the centre of the most concentrated sheep-farming area of the country. Land previously farmed by manorial custom was enclosed for pasture and grazing. Some peasants, now landless, were taken on as hired labourers. Many other peasants were without work, and gradually became known as the 'sturdy beggars' of a subsequent generation.

Oats became a major crop, needed for sheep-feed as well as the long-standing uses in bread-making and brewing.

Brewing, like all trades, was strictly controlled in medieval England. The Court of Bradford regulated this and every trade. Year on year, licences were issued to the brewers, and the very first

Figure 5. Market Cross, Bradford. *Bradford Libraries*

page of the Court Rolls lists the licensed brewers for 1339. The entries were almost indecipherable a century ago, but survive - minus forenames - in the translation made at that time:

Chapman
Raynery
of Thomas
of Robert
Attetounhend
Horton

Later in the same year, eighteen people are fined various amounts (all around 3d) for illegal brewing. (The same court found five people guilty of illegally practising the trade of shoemaker/tanner) The license to brew, specified in the court of 1354, was precisely worded:

> *William Perkin and Isabella his wife ... made fine with the lord for 16d for having license to brew and sell a gallon of ale at one penny until the feast of St Michael next to come so that they brew good ale*

*and sufficient at this price and that they sell their beer outside their
houses if asked by pottels and gallons and quarts.*

Bradford had its mill. As was usual at the time, ownership of the mill,
and regulations as to its use, were within the lease of the bailiwick.
Details of the renewal of the lease of the bailiwick were recorded in
the Rolls in 1357 and subsequently.

The tenancy of the manor of Bolling was also recorded. In 1361,
it was stated that 'Robert de Bolling holds the manor Bolling by
homage, scutage and knight service'. The cost to Robert was one
third of a knight's fee. This gives an indication of the comparative
value of Bolling: Allerton was held by the same feudal service but at
half a knight's fee.

There are numerous references to building work, but nearly always
in connection with maintenance of roads. This work was a public
duty, and always one to be avoided unless one was compelled by law
to comply. Sometimes however, it is obvious that wilful damage to a
road had been caused. People dumped their refuse and emptied their
cesspits along the roadside, and they stole stone, presumably for their
own building needs. So, for instance, in 1411, Thomas Dixon and
others were ordered to 'amend the highway at Horton Loyne, which
they damaged with seeking for clay.'

Leisure

The fourteenth century was a time of general and increasing poverty
for the whole country, and Bradford was in one of the poorest areas
of England. There was a Poll Tax in 1378-80, of which the records for
Bradford have survived. Those eligible to pay numbered 442 for the
whole Manor, and from this figure it has been estimated that the total
population, including children, the elderly, beggars, servants and
other such people who were not eligible to pay, would be around
1200. This total was divided among the various townships: the
population in North Bierley for instance would have been around
112.

In times of privation, feeding the family would have been a full-
time occupation. But even so, there is abundant evidence, not only of
leisure activities, but also of official disapproval of at least some of
those activities. By the early years of the next century, firm attempts
were made to suppress these:

*John Wilson of Manyngham [is] charged here in court for that he is
a common player of dice and other games prohibited, that is to say
kewdrynge, clockynge ....*

That some of the officials of the court connived at illegal gaming is clear:

> *John Wright of Bollynge, William Cottonlay...and William Newall...who were jurors of the vill of Bollynge (have) until the next court...to answer for that they concealed and would not present players of knucklebones within the vill there.*

The year 1412 was a year of sustained suppression of all revelry, including what at first may be surmised to be the equivalent of modern 'war games'. It was reported to the Court that:

> *John Tomlinson of Idle goes armed...with doublet de Fens, Wyrchatt, Karlehax and other unlawful arms,...and...has nothing whereby to live, goes well apparelled and will not work but is awake in the nights and asleep in the days.*

That was in May. Perhaps the 'doublet de Fens' was a protective coat worn when fencing, and the 'wyrchatt' may have been a 'wire shirt' or coat of mail. Perhaps too, this was not all games, but serious crime. In the following March:

> *Thomas Gibson, Thomas Rawson, Those Dixon, Adam Whitehead, Adam Bridge...continue to carry les Karlehaxes, les Pikestaves and go daily arrayed in doublet de Fens and Wyrechattes.*

Crime

If these men were engaged in criminal activities, they were not the only ones, for crimes of more serious nature were referred to a higher Court. The early days of the fourteenth century were times when what we would call today 'grievous bodily harm' was inflicted on a fairly regular basis. So frequent was it that it was dealt with in the Manor Court. In 1346, at Wibsey, there had been an affray of some kind: 'William son of Hugh drew blood of John de Aldoulegh [and of] Adam Jowett.' They, and a whole group of men. were fined for this. In fact, the south part of Bradford seems to have been a particularly violent area. A case was brought to court, also at Wibsey, later in the year, 'John son of Robert del Gille of Wybesay stole an ox, 6s, from Robert de Manningham at Roidsparke' and 'Adam del Park drew blood from William Milner of Birle'. Moreover, it was not only the menfolk who were violent: 'Cecilia del Olrehed of malice aforethought beat and ill-treated Margaret the wife of William de Whitacres to the shedding of blood and ... the aforesaid Cecilia is a common evil-doer.'

Figure 6. The punishment stocks at Baildon. *Bob Duckett*

There is no indication of what lay behind the following abduction from a house in Horton in 1353:

Thomas Sharp of Horton (is) charged with entering the house of Thomas of Northorp at Horton against his will and there did take with him and lead away from thence a certain Matilda his maidservant, by which the aforesaid Thomas has suffered loss and had damage to his affairs.

Apart from the many mentions of 'drawing blood', the fourteenth century equivalent of grievous bodily harm, there is only rarely in these court records a reference to serious crime. One example, however, deserves special mention. There is a long description of an incident that occurred in 1354 between the Vicar of Bradford and a parishioner in the wool trade:

> *...on Wednesday the eve of the Circumcision of our Lord in the 28th year of the reign of the now King, Sir Adam Boloure, chaplain, ...made his journey towards the tenterground of Bradford for the purpose of leaving his cloths there to be hung up and John Webster of Bradford, junior, advancing towards the church for the purpose of agreeing with the Vicar about a certain controversy existing between the same Vicar and his servants and William de Hornbi and him and the said John Webster met upon the bridge of Bradford. And then the aforesaid Sir Adam accosting the aforesaid John said to him, "Why have you called me a rogue?" who openly denied this. And then the said Sir Adam answering said to him rightly "Thou liest in thy head". And so leaping forward he drew out a certain knife called "Basetard", hanging to John Webster's girdle. And having drawn out the said knife he thrice struck the aforesaid John upon the shoulder so that the knife was broken. And then the aforesaid John, having drawn out a small knife called "Twistal", ran after the said Sir Adam and then the aforesaid Sir Adam...fell on his back and so lying, in his own defence, struck the aforesaid John with his feet twice; and then the aforesaid John struck the aforesaid Sir Adam, so lying, on his knee with the aforesaid small knife and so thereupon they departed.*

Serious crime, among the clergy or the laity, was rare. Petty crime, however, considering the size of the population of this little town, was high. In the same year, 1354, 'Ralph att Tounend, unjustly raised the hue at night.' Raising the hue was the calling out of the townfolk to pursue and apprehend a felon. To do so at night was a major inconvenience to the whole able-bodied population. To do so without just cause, or perhaps even as a prank, cost Ralph a fine of 12p. This was expensive fun! By comparison, breaking the licensing laws was only fined at the rate of 4p.

In 1357, the Court reached the end of its patience with one man:

> *Robert Dickson is a common quarreller and a common chider with his neighbours of Bradford and ... he generally harms the cattle of the lord's tenants passing through the plots of Bradford, therefore distrain him.*

Another conviction, with a fine of 9d each, was passed on 'Agnes Bascholf, Alice wife of Roger Watson and Dionisia wife of John Coke (who) were common disturbers of their neighbours'. They pleaded 'not guilty' but the court convicted them. A similar case was brought before the Court two years later, when Agnes and at least two other neighbours were at loggerheads: 'Christiana Jacdoghtre and Agnes Bascholf are common quarrellers with their neighbours'.

One matter that came before the court with almost monotonous regularity was the punishing of infringements of trade regulating rules. John Kirk and a whole list of others were fined 2d each in 1345 for 'brewing against the assize'. The following year, it is presumably John's wife who comes before the bench, along with others: 'The wife of John Attekirk, 2d, for brewing against the assize'. John and his wife appear regularly in the lists of those accused of illegal brewing. One can only assume that they regarded the 2d per annum fine as an expense, offsettable against profits.

Who's Who

Through the fourteenth century, Bradford gradually changed the way it referred to its inhabitants, thus following the practice that had become quite prevalent further south. By the time that Henry IV died, in 1412, surnames are no longer nicknames but family names. The process was nation-wide, but in the more populous south the process had begun earlier and progressed more quickly: once there are several Johns living at the Town End, or Williams living in Bierley, then more precise naming is called for.

Edward III was king when the first of Bradford's surviving Court Rolls begins. At that time, surnames were in existence, but rare. In 1345 there is list of illegal brewers, as mentioned above: it may seem that John Kirk had his surname as a family name, except that very soon afterwards the person who appears to be his wife is called 'wife of John Attekirk". Kirk is therefore interchangeable with Attekirk, and is a geographical description of John. He lived by the church. In the 1345 list where he appears, none of the other names appear to be family names.

Geographical names appear many times at this period:

John de Aldonlegh	1347
Robert del Gille of Wibsey	1348
Robert de Manningham	1348
Adam del Parke	1353
William Milner of Birle	1353
Cecelia del Olrehed	1354

Another very prevalent way of naming is by patronym:

William son of Hugh	1347
John son of Robert del Gille of Wibsey	1348
Thomas son of Adam son of Robert	1353
Alice daughter of John Gepson	1354
Christiana Jacdoghtre	1361

But the system could no longer cope. Change was necessary and social forces accelerated the change. Surnames, no longer as nicknames but surviving through the generations as family names, were coming more regularly into use. Infrequent in 1339, the earlist surviving court roll, they nevertheless appeared from time to time:

Adam Jowett	1348
Robert Cordingley	1348
Thomas Sharp	1353

Where there was no recognised family name, there were accepted ways whereby one could with precision identify a litigant or an accused. But they were becoming cumbersome:

John son of Robert del Gille of Wibsey	1348
Margaret the wife of William de Whitacres	1354
Thomas son of Elias of Bierle, smith	1357
Alice, widow of Henry atte Halle of Howarth	1362

In 1412, on the eve of Henry V's accession, surnames are the norm in Bradford: descriptive names or nicknames are the exception. Regular court appearances for petty crime are made by people with names such as Thomas Dixon, John Tomlinson, Thomas Gibson, and Thomas Rawson. The 'son of' has gone, and the spelling of Dixon indicates that no longer is Dick his immediate father. William Thornton, Adam Bridge and Thomas Rose are still there, but without the 'de' or 'del' indicating that they are described by their whereabouts.

Yet the old ways are not entirely gone. In 1413 John son of Thomas Walker of Bierley is still playing at knucklebones with Thomas Walker of Bierley and William son of John Newall of Park House. And again they are in court for it. Someone should have told them to post a lookout to warn them that the constable was coming!

Further Reading

A copy of the Manor Court Rolls may be consulted in the Local Studies Reading Room at Bradford Central Library.
Joseph Fieldhouse *Bradford*. 1972
Gary Firth *A history of Bradford*. Phillimore, 1997.
John James *A history and topography of Bradford*. 1861

2. THE TRAGEDY OF JERRY DELANEY – A BROOMFIELDS HERO

by Ronnie Wharton

BROOMFIELDS WAS A TRIANGULAR SHAPED AREA which had the Great Northern Railway as its western boundary and Wakefield Road as its eastern boundary. Broomfields terminated at the junction of Caledonia Street and Hall Lane at the point where the Wakefield Road tramline swung left. Edward, Guy, Bolling and Carter were the streets which run parallel with Wakefield Road, with Bedford, Chandos, Hardy, Broom and Granby streets running horizontally from the railway to the main road. (Figure 1)

In July 1935, compulsory purchase orders were served and in the

Figure 1. 1908 map of the Broomfields area of Bradford. *Bradford Libraries*

following year, after the confirmation of a Minister of Health order, the final demolition began on the adjacent-to-town slums belonging a row of streets as notorious as any in Bradford. The clearance of Broomfields and the moving of the residents to the delights of the Council's new show piece, Canterbury Estate, was the end of an era. (An often repeated story relates that the appearance of the new arrivals coincided with the disappearance of all the ducks on nearby Horton Park Lake.)

If legend is to be believed, the traumas of living in modern day Holmewood or Lower Grange seem trivial in comparison to the back-to-back world of Broomfields before and after the First World War. Heavily populated by second and third generation Irish families whose forefathers had moved to Bradford as an act of survival, the cheap near-to-town back-to-backs attracted some of the town's shady characters, as a sift through the local papers of the time can prove by the number of permanent fixtures in court. (Figure 2)

Being able to handle oneself in an area where in higher East Bowling one patrolling local 'bobby' was sufficient, but in lower Broomfields the 'boys in blue' went about in two's, three's or even four's, was a necessity. When it was learned, as it was in the years leading up to the turn of the century, you could legally earn money by turning your natural fighting aggression into becoming a professional boxer, Broomfields became a breeding ground of fistic talent. For in a twenty year span up to the commencement of the First World War, all within a hundred yard's locality, Broomfields produced Paddy Mahoney, the 8 stone 6 lb champion of England, 'Sticker' Atkinson, one of the leading boxers in the North, Fred

Figure 2. Looking down towards the Broomfields today. *Bob Duckett*

Delaney, a contender for the British Lightweight title and the best of the bunch, and Jerry Delaney who, but for tragic circumstances, could have been World Champion.

As well as fighters, Broomfields contained runners (not just bookies) and in Billy Hall, the only man ever to win both the Sheffield handicap and the Boothall plate, they boasted one of Bradford's finest.

Of the many boxing families to come out of Bradford, one family stands head and shoulders above the rest as the producer of an array of boxing talent which in the years before the First World War put Bradford boxing firmly on the map. The fact alone of producing six brothers who were capable of earning a living as professional boxers has probably only been rivalled once by the Moody family of Wales, who were reputed to have produced seven.

Famine and acute unemployment problems saw to a steady exodus from Ireland during the early part of the nineteenth century. The first landmark for the settlers in Bradford happened in 1825, when the Irish community had increased sufficiently to enable the construction of St Mary's, a catholic church in Stott Hill.

Quarter of a century later with regular job availability in an expanding woollen textile industry, the number of first generation immigrants had risen to 9,581, which was 8.3% of Bradford's population. (History was to repeat itself a century later when the first immigrants from Asia found the textile trade a steady employer). The figure of 9,581 was 26% of the total Irish born population in the West Riding. Leeds and Hunslet came next with 23%. Goit Side was the main Irish quarter, but living in central cheap housing had its drawbacks with the Irish children the weakest and most vulnerable in a lethal smoke polluted environment. During the 1850s and 60s, the death rate among the Irish was higher than that for the town as a whole, with Irish children making up half the deaths. Following on from Goit Side, Black Abbey and White Abbey, Nelson Street, Adelaide Street, the Wakefield Road end of Bedford Street and the streets of Broomfields became the later homes of the Irish and their second and third generations.

Born in Tipperary in 1833, William Delaney joined the growing army of disenchanted Irishmen who sought their fortunes elsewhere. Bradford was already a popular word back home and by the time the 1871 census was taken, Bradford had spread at an alarming rate to 147,101 population. Billy Delaney was among the one hundred and forty seven thousand, employed as a woolcomber and living in Wapping Road. The textile trade was notorious for long hours and low pay. As soon as the market slumped the first thing that dropped was workers' wages, but even low wages were acceptable when real poverty had been known. Billy's wife, Jane, became a weaver and his two lads, John and the three-year younger William, joined their father in the Bradford mills. The Delaney's clan was already spreading in Broomfields, with four families in the area at the 1871 census (two were in Granby Street and one each in Bolling Street and Broom Street).

Almost as a common a name as Delaney in the Irish quarter was Durkin. Born in Queens County, Ireland, in 1837, Catherine Durkin arrived in York in 1855. Within a year she had given birth to a daughter, Mary. Thomas and Anne followed, but by the time Catherine was born, the family had moved to Guy Street in Bowling. In the 1871 census, the head of the family, Catherine, was a worsted weaver, with fifteen year old Mary and ten year old Anne following suit. Nine year old Catherine was in school and now had two other sisters in Sarah, seven and Elizabeth, eight months. The family were still in Bowling nine years later when young Catherine walked down the aisle with Billy Delaney junior at St Mary's in June 1880. According to the marriage certificate, Catherine senior's husband, Johnny Durkin, had deceased, the younger Catherine had followed her sisters into the worsted mill, whilst in the Delaney family, who were now living in Windsor Street, the father had progressed to a carding overlooker and young Billy was looking after combing machines.

The move of the young couple to Broomfields coincided with the start of baptisms at the area's new Catholic church, St Anne's. Commencing with Edward in September 1881 the couple gave birth to 13 children in 23 years. Catherine's final child being Helina in April 1904 when she was aged 42. When two of the children died young, their names were given to later borns. The only time the births fell out of the two year cycle between them all was when following Frank, who was born in February 1891, Jerry was born on the last day of December 1892. The family's first home was in Broom Street, but by the time the majority of the children had been born, the Delaney's had spent a decade in Granby Street.

The boxing 'bug' began with second eldest brother, Jack, who became a more than useful bantamweight. Boxing at the turn of the century, he was a regular at the 'Rat Pit' in Ivegate. Billy (who boxed as Fred) and Jerry (younger than Billy by seven years) became national figures in the sport in the period up to the First World War. Sadly their Bradford appearances were limited, particularly in the case of Jerry, Bradford's only boxer of world championship class, who only appeared in the city in his very early days.

Frank, who was a year older than Jerry, appeared spasmodically. He fought a well remembered £20 aside clash with Kid Kelly, the Manningham based Army champion, and was reputed to have beaten Johnny Basham, the British Champion in an unrecorded fight.

Thirty years of boxing didn't stop there. With fighting in the blood, members of the next generation carried on scrapping with probably the best known being featherweight Tommy Madden, a nephew of the brothers.

From Newsboy to the National Sporting Club

The finest of the boxing Delaney brothers was undoubtedly Jerry (Figure 3). No disrespect to any later boxers who fought for titles, but Bradford has never produced better. The great tragedy of Jerry Delaney is that not only did the Great War rob Bradford of the chance of having a world title holder, it stopped us from knowing how great in the sport Jerry could have become in fulfilling the many expert predictions made about him.

After leaving St Anne's school in Broomfields, the youngster from Granby Street followed Billy's (Fred the elder) footsteps into a job as a newspaper seller of the *Bradford Daily Argus* and it wasn't long after before young Jerry was following his brother's footsteps in another direction. Broomfields was full of fighters of one sort or another and Jerry was only following a tradition of hungry fighters by donning the boxing gloves. When the local awareness of his potential came into being, there couldn't have been a better right hand than his brother Fred. In his ten years in the ring, Fred had fought the best lightweights in the country and it's a documented fact of the time that some of the hardest fights in Jerry's five year career

Figure 3. Jerry Delaney. *Boxing. R. Wharton*

were in the training ring with brother Fred.

After winning his first fight in spectacular fashion by a first round knockout, the power of Jerry's right hand punching guaranteed a run of quick wins and by 1911 Jerry had followed in the footsteps of Paddy and Sticker by becoming the new idol of Broomfields. (Fred had never become a street idol in the same sense, because for a big percentage of his fistic career he wasn't around). Whilst Jerry's reputation was quickly growing, Bradford had another young man with fistic talent and a likewise growing reputation in Fred Blakeborough.

At the opening night of Freckleton Wraith's new Bradford Sporting Club in March 1911, a full house of 1500 had witnessed the seventeen year old Blakeborough win a twenty round contest against Curly Osborne of London. Osborne was billed as the 7 stone 12 lb champion of England and a winner of two hundred fights.

The Osborne victory had made Blakeborough's reputation in the town and as a result of a series of challenges between the two fighters in the press, the youngsters met six months later at the Coliseum Rink, Toller Lane, in a fight fixed at £75 for the winner. Despite a drenching wet night, there was a tremendous attendance. 'Bus loads' had come through from around Granby Street and as soon as the doors had been opened the reserved seats had been rushed with the tickets on them conveniently left under the seats. Fred's seconds were Manningham based fighter Alf Wood, Fred's father Ben and his brother Will. (Perhaps overshadowed by Fred, Will moved to the North East when there was problems getting fights in Bradford. He accumulated an impressive list of victims including Irish bantam champion Billy Deane and Sheffield's Joby Jordon, who later held Jerry to a draw. During 1914, he fought in France, but sadly his name was added to the list of those killed in action whilst serving with the Bradford Pals in 1915 aged twenty two). In Jerry's corner were Sticker Atkinson, Sam Leach and Fred Delaney.

The referee was M.Murray, the editor of *Boxing*. To the onlookers it appeared a very close contest with Jerry edging it. There was no doubt in Murray's mind, on his card Jerry won 12 rounds, Fred four and four even. As the Delaney camp went their happy way back to Broomfields, no one had an inkling that they had seen Jerry's last big fight in Bradford.

The following year, the lads who earned their living from boxing in Bradford suffered a blow when the Chief Constable in the city announced that no licences to allow professional boxing in Bradford would be given. The Delaney's, who had at one time been based at

Figure 4. There is little left today that Jerry would recognize in his home street. *Bob Duckett*

the Castle and later moved over to Tom Maher's Packhorse, were even stopped training rights. Alderman Trotter 'put his penneth in' when he stated in a newspaper article early in 1912, that in regard to the recent boxing, he and many others were with the Chief Constable in his action. The ban was to last until March 1914. Ironically, only a couple of months after the March promotion, Bradford played host to a troupe of women boxers, who after being banned in other areas, were given an engagement at the Alhambra Theatre. That they were serious is in no doubt, for among the four boxers appearing were Marthe Carpentier (sister of the famous French boxer), the female boxing champion of the world, who had won the title by knocking out Miss Lucy Warner in four rounds in a recent fight held in Chantilly, France. Miss Carpentier issued a challenge in the local press for any budding female to take her on in the ring. Lucy Warner who had the title 'Lady Champion of England' was also on the bill.

Unable to fulfil his fighting ambitions in his hometown, Jerry moved to the North East, where he boxed a draw at South Shields with Johnny Robinson in a match for £25 a side. Jerry wasn't alone in the North East, the Blakeborough brothers found work there and with all three of them the lightweight range, they were able to 'compare notes' on opponents.

Despite barely two years experience, the fame and fortune of America was too big a 'carrot dangler' to resist. His brother's illness curtailed the Stateside trip and Jerry's only appearance was a thrilling six round no-decision contest against Bobby Scanlon in New York.

With good press reviews, there was the chance of staying on with every promise of making good. Family loyalty came first and with the ban still on in Bradford it was back to the North East for Jerry on his return.

Back in action in Newcastle, Jerry carried on where he had left off by stringing together several victories. Among the fights he won at the St James' Hall was a decisive win against Harry Sterling when odds of 11 to 8 were laid on Jerry. It was whilst he was in the North East that he had a most notable victory over the Frenchman Eugene Volaire. The Broomfielder outboxed his opponent for five rounds before falling to a left hook as he was about to finish his man. The blow had caught Jerry flush on the jaw and only Yorkshire grit enabled him to rise off the canvas to beat the count. While the Frenchman pursued him round the ring looking to land the killer punch, a brilliant display of defensive boxing brought the crowd to its feet. By the end of the round Jerry's sheer pluck was 'swinging the pendulum' back. In the next two rounds Volaire was punched to a standstill before he 'fouled out' to earn a seventh round disqualification ('fouling out', as the term was known, was a facet of boxing. When a boxer was on the verge of being beaten, he deliberately earned a disqualification which didn't look as bad as a knockout or a 'referee stopped fight' decision on his record).

News of this outstanding boxer travelled quickly and by March 1914 Jerry was engaged at the famous National Sporting Club, the headquarters of boxing. (Jerry's Bradford rival Fred Blakeborough had made the capital after a string of successive victories, but didn't have that extra class to earn a title shot. He lost a close points decision to Con Houghton, the ex-amateur feather champion, in an eliminator for a crack at Ted Kid Lewis, the British Champion. Seaman Hayes stopped him in the later stages after Fred had built up a good lead and in a second eliminator, Jerry, who was Fred's second, was forced to throw in the towel when Fred had gone down twice in the tenth round against Llew Edwards).

Jerry's London appearance was most impressive and in a completely one-sided fight he easily disposed of Brighton's Danny Hughes. A month before the Hughes fight, Jerry had made an appearance at Birmingham where he had outclassed 'Brummie' fighter Jack Ward, flooring him several times before a tenth round knockout. The Bradford lad had so won over the Midlands fans that the Birmingham promoter had no hesitation in booking Jerry again, this time against his best opponent to date, Willie Farrell. The match was fixed for £100 a side plus purse and at 9 Stone 9lbs or under. Whilst Jerry had no problems making the weight, Farrell weighed in at 10 Stone 3lbs and was extremely annoyed at having to forfeit £75 for being over the fixed weight. The legendary Jim Driscoll, through his friendship with Jerry's older brother Fred, was now taking an interest in the younger Delaney, and old 'Peerless' had no hesitation in telling his man to take the fight and ignore the weight advantage. Despite the forfeit, Farrell's backers were confident of making a bob or two from the fight, but what a shock for them and what a disappointment for the packed house when the fight was all over inside two rounds. Delaney's accurate hitting had Farrell down in the first round and three times in the second before the referee had no alternative but to stop it because Farrell was unable to defend himself. Farrell immediately clamoured for a return, claiming he wasn't fit for the fight and stating he was overweight because he was unable to train due to an ankle injury.

During the same period, Jerry made what was for him rare appearances in Yorkshire by fighting twice at Carlton Hill Barracks in Leeds. In the first one against George Ruddick of Leeds, fixed for £180 a side stake and purse, Jerry had so outclassed his man by the third round that it was a forgone conclusion, but surprisingly the referee prolonged it till round six when a towel was thrown in. Nine year old Fred Delaney was at ringside for Jerry's second Leeds appearance. Going to Leeds for a youngster before the First World War was like going to London. Fred struggled to remember the fight later in life, but what did stand out in his memory was on that day Jerry had beaten a Frenchman. Backstreet youngsters in 1913 had never seen a 'Frenchie', so young Fred always had a crowd round

Figure 5. The once populous Irish quarter of Broomfileds is now 'urban desert'. *Bob Duckett*

when he related the tale of 'how our Jerry gave the Frenchman a good hiding!' Fernard Quendreux wasn't in the same class and was well beat by the time the contest ended in the sixth round.

Jerry's latest round of success brought another engagement at the National Sporting Club. The matchmaker at boxing's headquarters was looking for an opponent to face the American Harry Stone. Newly arrived in this country, the New Yorker had a reputation as one of the best lightweights in America. (Previous to his England visit Stone had beaten the best in Australia, including top British fighters Johnny Summers, whom he beat twice, and Matt Wells, who were both touring there). Still unbeaten, Jerry was chosen as the man to try and put this cocky and extrovert American in his place. At the weigh in before the fight, Stone smoking a huge black cigar of overpowering strength tried to make the ceremony a mockery by saying it was hardly worth bothering to put the gloves on for the one punch it needed to beat his opponent. He even went as far as to ask Jerry whether he would not rather call the fight off and so save himself 'the father and mother of a hiding'. When the American loudmouth had left the smoke filled scaleroom, leaving a parade of choking and eye-watering onlookers, one wondered if the matchmaker had given young Jerry too daunting a task. The crowd were still apprehensive when Stone entered the ring smoking another of his horrible cigars. Wearing a cloth cap and a dressing gown of many vivid colours, the colourful American behaved in the corner as if it were a waste of time putting on the gloves just for the one punch needed. Trying not to look overawed, Jerry knew the American wouldn't have lasted two minutes with a partisan crowd back home; his brash attitude would have had the local clan baying for blood. The National Sporting Club were much more refined, but they were shown to be a bit more boisterous than usual when Stone rushed at Jerry with bull-at-a-gate tactics to try and justify his early predictions. When Delaney, cooly sidestepped him and clipped his rival with a sting as he went floundering past, the crowd were right behind the Yorkshireman.

Jerry then proceeded to give the American a boxing lesson and outclassed and outboxed him in every round. Stone changed his tactics at various stages of the fight, but he was no match for young Delaney who withstood his every manoeuvre. Realising he had little to fear from the American, Jerry brought the crowd to their feet with a show of straight lefts, hooks, jabs and right uppercuts and it was only remarkable gameness that enabled Stone to be on his feet at the finish. Stone knew that he had been beaten by a better man and swallowed his American pride to be the first to give the victor a hearty congratulations. (Stone was around for a while. Llew Edwards the British and British Empire Featherweight champion from 1915-17 had six clashes with him. Llew lost only thirteen in an over-100 fight career and four of them were against Stone. The American went twenty rounds with Ted Kid Lewis, the World Welterweight champion, in New Orleans).

In the euphoria of Delaney's great win, the acknowledged experts were tipping a great future for the Bradford lad and already comparisons were being drawn with Jim Driscoll and the World Champion, Welshman Freddie (real name Freddie Thomas) Welsh.

Welsh had recently won the world title from American Willie Ritchie in London, and immediately a suggestion was made that he should give Jerry a chance at his title. Welsh was said to be willing to fight Delaney for the title but he wanted a little breathing space. The Welshman had been a spectator at the Stone fight and though he made a promise to fight Jerry in six months, maybe he realised Jerry was a real threat, for he soon 'took his hook' over to America to look for more lucrative offers from American promoters.

The Somme - The Final Round
Within a fortnight of the Stone fight, the Great War had started. Jerry, as indeed did many other British boxers, volunteered immediately for active service. Being in reach of a world title fight was put second to patriotism and Jerry enlisted in the Sportsman's

Battalion. Brothers Jack, Frank and Joe also joined to serve, with the Delaney father proudly adding his name later.

Whilst in training prior to shipment to France there was time for two more contests in London. Following in the wake of Harry Stone, came another American with the show business trimmings. Claiming an overwhelming record, Jack Denny strutted into London with the proclamation that he wanted to meet the best we could offer. With the Stone fight still fresh in memory, the National Sporting Club matchmakers looked no farther. Jerry was able to obtain the necessary leave and the punters had another boxing feast in store. It was another classic performance from the Broomfields' idol. Denny had been expected to give Delaney a run for his money, but only by consistent covering did the American manage to survive until the fourteenth round when his seconds through in the sponge. Denny had certainly met the best the country could offer; he was so outboxed that he never laid an effective punch the whole fight.

Two months later, Delaney fought at the famous club in Covent Garden for the last time. Time was running out for the draft to France and Jerry used up leave time in which he could have journeyed home to give Willie Farrell another chance. Since the debacle of their first fight, Farrell had sought to wipe the slate clean. Willie had always stuck to the tale he had been unlucky in their first meeting, and with Jerry already the Sporting Club's firm favourite, there was no problem in guaranteeing another full turnout for the return. To give Farrell his due, he was worth another chance, and the Bradford soldier's opponent put up a great performance in going the full 20 rounds. What was on show was another masterful performance from Jerry Delaney. Every technique was there for the crowd's approval. Close punching, long range jabbing, footwork and feints that made the audience purr with delight were paraded to such a degree of expertise, that despite Willie putting up the fight of his career, Jerry was a comfortable points winner. The stalwarts of the National Sporting Club, eager for Jerry to be matched with Welsh, cabled the Welshman in America warning him that unless he defended his title against the official challenger, the lightweight crown would be declared vacant and Delaney would be given first chance to fight for it.

Jerry knew that he was due to go abroad the next draft. When there was talk of officials interposing on his behalf so that he could stay at home waiting the champion's return, the Bradfordian decided his duties were with the lads on the front line. There was just time to squeeze in one more fight, when Jerry met Jack Greenstock at

Liverpool in May 1915. Unfortunately it wasn't another classic. The fight produced little boxing due to the persistent holding and clinging by his opponent. Eventually by the seventh round the referee had had enough of these tactics and Greenstock was disqualified. No one was to know that Jerry had made his last appearance in the ring and as Jerry went over on the next draft, his proud record stood at 35 fights unbeaten (four of his 35 fights were draws. The Bobby Scanlon fight in New York was no contest whilst J. Robinson, Joby Jordan and Nat Williams got draw verdicts against him).

Jerry went on the next draft as planned and was soon in the front line. After a few months of trench warfare, Lance Corporal Jerry Delaney was awarded the Distinguished Conduct Medal. After spending days cooped up in dug outs, Jerry and his squad mates were part of a dawn raid party over No Man's Land. Laden with Mills bombs, the plan was to drive the Germans back into their reserve trenches. The party had hardly moved out of their starting blocks when a hail of bullets began to cut them down. Star shells illuminating the sky made the soldiers easy targets and the continuation of the mission foolhardy. With men dropping like ninepins, the command was reluctantly given to retreat. Running for his life, Jerry 'copped' for a bullet in the leg and another ripped through his sleeve. As he struggled back, the boxing soldier noticed a fellow colleague, one who had befriended him before going 'over the top'. Ignoring his injuries, Jerry carried the unconscious soldier over his shoulder back to the lines. For the action (9 January, 1915), Jerry was awarded the Distinguished Conduct Medal (Figure 6).

His gallantry award was well received back in Bradford. The concern over his injuries turned to relief when it was learned that his boxing career wouldn't be

Figure 6. 'Jerry Delaney brings in a pal from No-Man's-Land and wins a DCM.' *Boxing News*

curtailed and the great fighter could still nurse his unfilled ambition.

When they heard about his injuries, the City's boxing entrepreneurs, Messrs Holloway, Coyle (still active in the sport since his early association with Paddy Mahoney), Embleton and landlord of the Brownroyd Hotel, Jack Midgley, put on a benefit at the Palace for Jerry. Old rival Fred Blakeborough, a Lance Corporal in the 20th West Yorkshire, left his instructor duties at Catterick to come and take part in an exhibition with Kid Eastwood. The occasion was highlighted by the appearance of the 'boy wonder' Alfie Hebblethwaite. (Poor Alfie, in the not too distant future they would be having a benefit for him. Not a war victim, because Alfie was too young for that, but a victim of unscrupulous promoters who had him burned out after well over a century of ring fights whilst still in his teens).

After attention to his leg, Jerry refused a physical training instructor position which would have guaranteed him a journey back to England and the prospect of more fights. Back in 'Blighty' he was a boxing hero, but in the trenches he was a soldier who wanted no differential treatment from the rest of the boys on the front line.

Just over six months after his decoration, Jerry was one of the volunteers in a bombing raid at Delville Wood on the Somme. Fate decided he had answered his last bell as he was cut down on No Man's Land.

British boxing, still reeling after losing middleweight champion Tom McCormick only a few weeks before, paid Jerry the honour in a tribute in *Boxing* by likening him to Sir Arthur Conan Doyle's legendary hero 'Champion Harrison': 'the man who had never won the big title, but who was nevertheless so known and styled by his fellow ring heroes'.

Though he was buried in France, he wasn't forgotten. Lord Lonsdale headed a subscription which reached a few hundred pounds and a memorial was built in Bowling Cemetery (Figure 7). On that memorial are the words 'erected by friends and admirers of a brave soldier and noted boxer'. To bring the story more up to

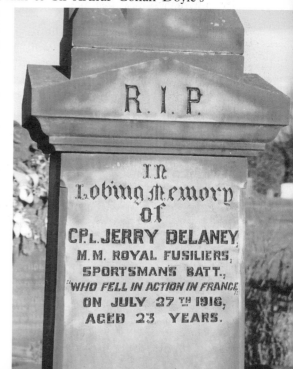

Figure 7. Jerry Delaney's memorial in Bowling cemetery. *Bob Duckett*

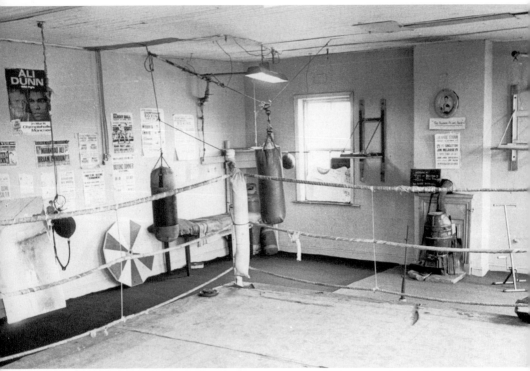

Figure 8. The 'Ali-Dunn' poster on the wall of the gym in the Farmyard Inn, Bowling Back Lane in 1976, provides an interesting link between Bradford's first British boxing champion, Richard Dunn, and the Broomfield' hero that so nearly was, Jerry Delaney. *Telegraph & Argus*

date, in 1960, noted Bradford sportsman T.E. Murgatroyd and the members of the Leeds and Bradford ex-professional boxers association, produced a brochure and held a concert at the Engineers Club in Westgate to raise money to lay a wreath and have the monument restored.

Sports writers talk a lot about quality. One thing for certain is that Jerry was in that bracket, and to be tragically wiped out when only in his early twenties, his full potential possibly not extended, with a world title within his grasp, was for the Bradford public 'a bitter pill to swallow'.

It is fitting that Bradford's greatest boxer has deservedly become a legend in sporting circles in his own town and that Jerry's name is not far from anyone's lips when some of the old timers reminisce on Bradford boxing. (Figure 8)

3. THORNTON VILLAGE

by Barbara Whitehead

LIKE ALL GROWING CITIES, BRADFORD has reached out to embrace nearby settlements. A hundred years ago the village of Thornton became officially part of Bradford. Bit by bit the outskirts of the city have crept closer, and new housing has expanded the village itself. Yesterday when I was out walking the dogs along Back Lane, which is in parts as pretty as any Cotswold village and has a delightful view over the countryside, I saw this dreaded notice on a green and ancient field, 'Building land for sale'.

So what is there still to Thornton to make it special?

The villages built on the flanks of the Pennine hills have a family likeness, whether they are Hebden Bridge, Haworth, Thornton or any one of a hundred others. Created out of the layers of stone they stand on, ignoring the steepness of their hillsides, they have a tough, down-to-earth look. Mixtures of styles and periods are blended by the strong local traditions of vernacular building, so that the individual houses are often difficult to date. The fashionable details one finds in town buildings are usually absent.

Like Haworth, Thornton has a magic ingredient; a connection with the Brontë family. 'Who are the Brontës?' I was asked recently by a travel agent. 'They are the most famous family of writers Britain has ever bred,' I answered, 'and they were born in Thornton'. No one in this part of Yorkshire is ever likely to forget that, if only because the name Brontë is used by so many businesses in the area.

Thornton lies on the south-facing slope of a wedge of high ground, some four miles west of the centre

Figure 1. Abandoned farm machinery, Headley Lane.
Richard Newman

of Bradford. This southern aspect is an advantage to many of the houses, as is the slope, for tier upon tier of them can look out over the pretty valley and catch the sun in their windows. At the time the Brontë family lived here, the industries of the place were small-scale. They were coal mining in the valley and stone quarrying on the higher ground and hilltops behind, together with agriculture and the cottage spinning of wool and weaving of cloth.

The stone, known locally as 'Delf', was used for everything in Thornton, from the cobbles underfoot to the 'grey slates' on the roofs overhead. In the Victorian period it was also exported far and wide. Where they have been cleaned, the stone walls here are light golden brown, but dark grey where past industrial and domestic smoke still blackens them.

There are many places in England called Thornton; often it is only part of the name. Roughly, it means, 'the enclosure (or homestead) amongst the thorn trees.' The spelling in the eleventh century

Figure 2. Alderscholes Lane. *Richard Newman*

Figure 3. Audrey and Arthur Brown, retired farmers. Thornton Hill Farm.
Richard Newman

Doomsday Book varied. Thornton could be spelt Torentone, Torintune, or Torrentun, and so on. The capital T would be pronounced 'th'.

After this early start, Thornton remained a thinly settled upland parish, the number of people increasing only very slowly. On the recreation fields at the top of the village, just above the *Sun Inn*, you can still see the wide ridges and furrows left by medieval ploughing. What grain was grown in Thornton would be mainly oats, used for thin flat oatcakes (haver bread) and porridge. These were basic foods of the people. Horses and donkeys provided the transport. In more modern times farming here is pastoral, with grazing animals. There are a lot of horses. Also sheep and cows, producing wool and mutton, milk and beef.

Figure 4. Cockin Lane, railway overbridge (now demolished). *Richard Newman*

By the seventeenth century the whole of the West Riding was starting to grow industrially. The coal mining in Thornton was mentioned in 1638. There was a wave of building throughout the area. Many of the halls and manor houses date from this time, or were enlarged then. In Thornton we still have some beautiful examples left, Headley Hall for instance, Thornton Hall and a number of others less outstanding.

During this time, small producers of cloth were taking their finished pieces to the growing towns to sell, either on their shoulders or on a donkey or horse, walking along the pack-horse trails which connected manor houses and villages. You can still trace many of the packhorse routes, there are several still used as footpaths round Thornton. One crosses the golf course in the valley at the south, another runs beside the recreation ground to the north.

One indicator of high business activity was the opening of the West Riding Register of Deeds at Wakefield in 1704, the first ever in the country. It was followed soon after by the opening of a Register of Deeds for Middlesex.

Slowly the little old settlements were becoming villages, Thornton, Denholme, Clayton, and the land was being enclosed and tamed. The cottages had always had their bit of land attached, the toft (or croft) where people could stretch their cloth on tenter frames, keep a pig or a few hens, grow vegetables. The tofts stretched uphill or down towards the river in the valley. Outside these were the open fields which gave rise to those wide ridge and furrow patterns, privately owned in strips but cultivated communally. Then there were the commons where the animals could graze and the 'waste' land, blending into the rugged wild moors around.

When I was standing on the golf course the other day and looking across the stream towards Thornton, I thought the narrow fields

Figure 5. Horses at Hill Top. *Richard Newman*

running parallel from the village towards the beck might possibly be the old tofts. I remembered that friends of mine had been surprised to find when they bought a house looking over the valley that the property included one of these narrow holdings. Looking down at my feet, I became convinced that the golf course itself was probably the site of one of the open fields, with the ridge and furrow pattern still faintly visible.

In 1771 the commons and waste lands of Thornton, 1600 acres, were enclosed. Walls were built round the amalgamated holdings and roads were laid out.

You may wonder what relevance the tofts, crofts and fields of long ago have to modern Thornton, but the layout of the conservation core of the village owes everything to those far-off days. The little alleyways between the houses were once paths across fields, the strangely shaped houses are that way because of old field boundaries. Once someone sold a fragment of their toft for someone else to build a house, and there the house still is today. In another place a whole field was sold, and a row of back-to-back houses built on it, or two facing terraces.

The Brontë family came to live in Thornton in 1815 and moved on

Figure 6. The Old Bell Chapel and Churchyard. *Richard Newman*

Figure 7. Thornton street sign. *Richard Newman*

to Haworth in 1820. These years were at a turning point in our history. The long war with the French finally ended in 1815, and was followed by years of austerity due to bad harvests. At the same time the development of industrial processes was speeding up and comunications improving. They were dramatic times.

The new Irish curate, Patrick Brontë, and his Cornish wife Maria became part of the top layer of society in the village and made friends with the local doctor's family, who lived at Kipping House, an elegant building largely dating from 1796. Now a much-loved home, Kipping House presents its back to the road. Like a number of houses in Thornton, its grander front faces its garden and the south view.

Maria Brontë, who had been brought up in the Methodist church, had her own income of £50 a year, much more than most working people could earn. Patrick had his stipend from the Church of England. They both wrote, although only Patrick's work was published, and they both had keen social consciences and did what they could to improve conditions for the people of the parish. When they arrived they already had two little daughters, Maria and Elizabeth, and went on to have more children at the rate of almost one a year, Charlotte, Branwell (the cherished only son), Emily Jane and Anne. All Mrs Brontë's babies lived. She had servants and nursemaids to help her run the busy house.

Figure 8. Thornton village. Street sign. *Richard Newman*

This rapid increase in the Brontë family was following the national trend, which we know from the census figures. In 1811 the population of Patrick's large parish had been 3016, and by 1821 it was 4100, so during the ten years convering the residence of the Brontë family there was continual growth resulting in an increase of a third in that time. In 1821 the 4100 people of the parish formed 796 families, average size 5.3 people, living in 788 houses, spread over four villages and several hamlets[1].

The house the Brontës lived in is now called The Brontë Birthplace and is 72/74 Market Street. We do not know its exact age, but the datestone of 1802 is the date it was modernised, enlarged and turned into a gentleman's residence. In 1807 it was sold to the Church of England as a house for the clergyman, together with the cottage at the side, the yard at the back with a small building for one horse and one cow, a garden in the shape of a triangle running up the hillside, and two flower beds at the front, one on either side of the front door. You can see the house today, marked by a plaque on the front wall with the names of the famous children born here. To a limited extent it is open to the public, and the basic layout is unchanged since the Brontë's day. Under a skimming of modern plaster lie their walls plastered with lime and animal hair, and under the modern plasterboard ceilings there are still their ceilings of lath and plaster. Three fireplaces survive from their day, including one splendid cast iron grate which would be the first to provide warmth for the new born infants.

Changes have of course taken place in the house, but it is being restored to the Regency style of the Yorkshire countryside. The biggest change was when in 1898 one of the flower beds was built on to form a butcher's shop. Many people in the village remember buying their meat at this shop. The little building at the back for 'one horse and one cow' was superseded by a large Victorian barn which has now been converted to a house.

The Church of England was not the biggest religious community in the parish, this was the non-conformist congregation of Kipping Chapel. Originally they met in a large, probably medieval, barn which still exists in Lower Kipping Lane. It has a wonderful roof and is potentially a magnificent building, but is in a sad state now. If it is allowed to become a ruin Thornton will have lost one of its greatest glories.

The present congregation meets in a handsome chapel on Market Street. There is also a strong Methodist community in the village.

When the Brontë family moved to Haworth, the tradition is that they had seven carts for their household furnishings and a wagonette

Figure 9. Thornton Public Baths, Spring Holes Lane. *Richard Newman*

Figure 10. Thornton viaduct. *Richard Newman*

Figure 11. Winter trees at Pinch Beck. *Richard Newman*

for the parents, children and nursemaids. Certainly there is documentary evidence for a neighbour having lent them one flat cart; this would hardly have been enough for all their household goods. Presumably other carts and a wggonette were hired, but the exact number cannot be known. Luckily it was spring. The horses pulled the cavalcade up to Hill Top and then on to Denholme and so over the moorland roads to Haworth, a higher and more exposed village. The journey was about six miles. In slightly later times the Haworth football team used to travel down to Thornton to matches with the local lads of Thornton or Clayton, who went to Haworth for return matches.

If you travel to Thornton by the B6145, from the Odeon corner in Bradford (the Odeon is next to the Alhambra), you are travelling on the turnpike road built in the eighteen twenties. If the Brontës had moved a little later, they would have driven by this road, but they would have had to stop now and then to pay a toll for access to the next stretch.

By this time, when communications were better, the cloth mills began to be built, the first in 1826. That mill was only semi-mechanised and was still labour intensive. Others followed, fully mechanised. The workers' houses began to go up. Middle-class tenants also lived in terrace housing. Halifax developed before Thornton as a textile centre and the cottages climbing the hill by the Brontë Birthplace were at first called 'New Halifax.' Now they are called Havelock Square, with strange little Havelock Street higher up. Once the mills arrived there was no need for the big cottage windows, and the workers would not have time for the agricultural activities of the tofts and crofts.

For a century the mills were prosperous, but few remain today. You can see Prospect Mill beside the B6145 (Thornton Road), now used for craft workshops and the rehearsal place for a team of acrobats. Further along the B6145 is South Square, once a dozen cloth-workers cottages and now housing an art gallery, vegetarian cafe, various craftsmen and women, and the nicest public toilets in Thornton. Further on still is the Wellington pub, named in the days when the Duke of Wellington, who beat Napoleon at Waterloo, was public hero number one. Now there is only one textile mill still working as such in Thornton, Downes Coulter & Co. Ltd, on West Lane.

New transport had arrived with the mills. Across the valley to the south strides a magnificent golden viaduct, unused since the Beeching axe chopped off this small railway from the trunk routes. The busy goods yards and marshalling yards have gone, but the railway viaduct in its solitary state is still with us. The builders of the pyramids could not have created their monuments with more pride than the builders of this splendid structure. Also from the railway era is the *Great Northern* pub at the edge of Thornton, built at the junction of old and new, the turnpike road and the railway.

Market Street, the heart of the village community, has, like so many shopping streets, felt the wind of change from out-of-town supermarkets. Even worse, the church school is to close, and the children, now so near to home, will have to make an awkward and tiresome journey.

In Market Street the shop windows are now mostly the fronts of dwelling houses. There are a few shops still. Amongst them are a general store, a dentist, a baker with the charming Brontë Tea Room, and a splendid pet shop which sells amongst other animals snakes

Figure 12. Wrought ironwork, Back Lane. *Richard Newman*

and lizards. Nearby on Kipping Lane there is the Post Office and an excellent butcher whose uppermost windows are the design which the Brontë family's bedroom windows once were. There are two hairdressers, and other commercial concerns. Towards the east end of Market Street are the library and the doctors' surgery. But in general Market Street is slumbering. Quaint and oldfashioned, its cobbles unfortunately covered by tarmac, it has narrow little cobbled roads leading from it. Cars emerge like rabbits from rabbit holes. From Back Field, for instance, endless cars also rock down the uneven cobbles of Havelock Square.

At present Market Street represents opportunity for the new millenium, created by the sadness of decline. It may return to the liveliness and promise of the days when it was the birthplace of literary genius. Perhaps one day speciality shops will give it the air of a Bond Street near Bradford.

Have I told you anything about Thornton, after all? I have not told you of the magical views between the houses, the freshness of the air up on the playing fields, the grimness of bad weather when rain-water streams in rivers down the hillside, the mixture of litter and loveliness, the dominant nature of the spire of St James' church or the romantic ruin which was once Patrick Brontë's Bell Chapel.

I have not told you of the way, after dark, that Market Street can take on the mysterious and haunting air of a Victorian street in a television drama. I have not told you about all the groups and societies which flourish here, or the bored youngsters who gather together and talk in the most unlikely and uncomfortable corners. I have not told you that there are probably more dogs per head of population than anywhere else I have lived, or that at six on a summer morning you can linger on the playing fields and watch the sun rise over Bradford. Any evening from almost any point in the village you can revel in the sunset, and on a clear night in tiny Thornton Park you can delight in the view of the stars.

Reference

1. These last statistics on number of people per house, and various other points, from T. Franks typescript (in Bradford Reference Library) *Urban Growth In Thornton*

The Brontë Birthplace, Thornton. *Drawing by Terry Roberts.*

4. A Sorcerer's Apprentice: Pharmacy in Pre-War Shipley

by Alex Robinson

MONDAY 23 AUGUST, 1932. I REMEMBER THE DATE WELL, the day I started work. A few minutes before 9 a m I entered the doors of the pharmacy of W.Rimmington Ltd, 31 Otley Road, Shipley. It stood at the 'Fox Corner', where the Leeds to Keighley and the Bradford to Otley roads intersect. That morning I started a career in pharmacy which lasted over sixty years, for it was not until 1997 that I finally gave up my last part time job and fully retired.

I did not want to be a pharmacist. I had just passed my Higher

Figure 1. Rimmington's of Shipley, on the left, at Fox Corner. *J.Norman Preston*

School Certificate - equivalent of today's A Levels - in chemistry, maths and physics, after six years at the old Salt Boys' High School at Saltaire. I had gone there with a County Minor Scholarship in 1926, quite an achievement for a lad with a poor background. We were poor; my father ended his working life as a labourer on the sewage works then under construction at Esholt, the village where we lived. I was the youngest of a family of six, and the first to get a scholarship for higher education. How my parents managed to keep me at secondary school for six years I'll never know, but they did.

I did well at school, was drawn to the sciences, and when the headmaster talked about a career I said I fancied working in a laboratory. Bradford's involvement in wool and the fact that our family was textile orientated - my father worked in a mill until an accident damaged his sight, and three brothers worked for big textile merchants - gave me a leaning towards a textile laboratory, perhaps in dyeing. 'For that you'll need a degree, Robinson,' declared the

Head. When I explained that attendance at University or college was out of the question he asked if I had considered pharmacy? I could get in by serving an apprenticeship.

I was terribly shy, and the thought of working behind a shop counter frightened me. Still, it was a job that involved chemistry, and if I could get in, it would be employment; I would give it a try.

To digress a moment; jobs, in 1932, were not easy to get. We had not fully recovered from the slump conditions of the 1920s which had led to three million folk 'on the dole' and hardships all round. Our own family was hit; two brothers were thrown out of work when their firm, old established Charles Semon & Co, went bust. A third brother was in an insecure position; textiles were in a bad way, mills on short time. It was not a time to hope for a job in the wool trade. It made sense to look for a position in a chemist's shop.

We call them 'Pharmacies' nowadays. We used to call them 'Chemists' or 'Chemists and Druggists', a name I prefer and shall use from now on. It has a more romantic ring to it. Towards the end of my schooldays I saw this notice in the Bradford *Telegraph and Argus*: 'Smart boy wanted as apprentice in high class chemist's'. I applied and was gratified to receive an invitation to be interviewed by Mrs Rimmington. She was the owner of W.Rimmington's, not to be confused with the famous firm, F.M.Rimmington of Bradford. This Shipley shop had been set up by Whitworth Rimmington in the early 1900s. It was well known and had this excellent position on a central corner (Figure 1).

Mr Rimmington had died a few years earlier. It was popularly supposed that his end had been hastened by indulgence in alcohol. The shop had a licence to sell wines and spirits, and Whitworth had sampled his wares freely. I was given to understand that, the firm being in a rocky state, his death could have been providential.

Mrs Rimmington was rather unusual. She called on me to attend her residence for interview on a Saturday evening of all times. She was small and fussy and talked for about an hour, hardly asking me a question. She had telephoned the school and got a glowing report from the Head, which was good enough for her. She told me they would send for me in August.

I would be paid a wage; ten shillings a week for the first year, fifteen shillings the second year, and one pound a week for the last year of a three year apprenticeship. I did have a look at the shop and an interview with the bosses - two of them. The manager was quite elderly, Mr Dwyer, a delightful chap. He had joined the firm at the start as an unqualified assistant. He had served an apprenticeship at York but had never bothered to go to college and qualify. He knew it all, was a business man, did the books, and carried the firm through difficult days.

To keep a chemist's shop you had to have a qualified person (an MPS) on the premises. The chemist at Rimmington's was a middle-aged Jew from Leeds. It was an unfortunate situation; a qualified man does not like taking orders from an unqualified person; in turn, the unqualified man, with a lifetime of experience, is going to resent the fact that a less experienced, less knowledgeable man has the advantage of a certificate of qualification and the powers that go with it. Mrs Rimmington warned me she was aware of friction; it was up to me to be diplomatic and keep a balance. Just another little duty for a good apprentice!

First Impressions

That was the background to my starting work at Rimmington's, a real old-fashioned chemist's. Mahogany shelves and fittings; behind the counter a range of mahogany faced drawers with white glass labels, bearing names of contents in Latin (Figure 2). Fruct Senna, Flor Anthem, Sem Lini (Senna Pods, Camomile Flowers and Linseed!). On shelves above were rows of elegant glass bottles with ground glass stoppers - 'shop rounds' to us. Some were in deep blue glass with wide necks and heavy stoppers (Figure 3). These were designed for thick syrups - Sennas, Orange and Figs. Clear glass bottles housed tinctures, infusions, spirits. Again, all had white labels edged with gold and red, declaring contents in Latin. Customers said that was to hoodwink them, so they had no idea what was going into their bottle of medicine, 'It's tradition' was our reply. (Figure 4)

I have always been afraid of being late so I was standing outside Rimmington's door at 8.30 that Monday morning. It was nearly 9 o'clock before someone came to let me in. This was the senior apprentice, a smart young man called Leslie Brewer, who was just coming to the end of 'his time', and would leave at Christmas. 'You coming to work here?' he asked. 'I thought so, nobody tells me anything. I didn't know a new apprentice was starting. Come on in here!' and led me round the back of the counter into a back room - workshop and office and store. A broad counter ran down the middle of the room, evidently a work table. Underneath it held an array of pestles and mortars, pans, glass and metal measuring jugs. The walls were lined with shelves carrying reserve stocks. In one corner was an old roll-top desk, Mr Dwyer's office domain. At the far end of the room was a fireplace and what had been a kitchen range. At

Figure 2. '... a range of mahogany-faced drawers with white glass labels, bearing the names of contents in Latin.' *Salts Estates*

sometime in the past owners had lived behind the shop.

A first impression as I tried to take everything in was the smell - the chemist shop smell. I can just recall it in my 'nasal memory', no longer with me in actual fact for with over-exposure I lost it long ago. A great pity for it was one of the great attractions of the chemist's. An aroma compounded of scented soaps, herbs, spices, spirits, camphorated and other oils and goodness knows what, that indefinable perfume touched with chemicals that declared a chemist's shop. Friends used to tell me 'I smelt of the chemist's!' That was all right, I smelt good whatever my looks.

Back in the back room, Leslie asked me if I'd brought an overall, indicating that if I was going to work I'd better look ready for it when Mr Dwyer arrived, an event Leslie predicted would be at one minute to nine. I had been surprised to be admitted by a junior, I thought only a manager would have keys to a chemist's shop.

Figure 3. 'Elegant glass bottles'. *Salts Est*

I put on my brown shop coat ready for action. This had been an early surprise, Mr Dwyer advising me to report for duty bringing a brown or grey shop coat to work in. I had thought chemists worked in white coats. Why should I have a coloured one? Mr Dwyer said I looked smart when he came in with a cheery greeting dead on one minute to nine. Two minutes before

Figure 4. 'All had white labels edged with gold and red, declaring contents in Latin.' *Salts Estate*

that a tall, ginger-haired youth, a bit younger than me (I was then seventeen) had dashed in, gone to an outer back room called 'the warehouse', and armed with brush and shovel started vigorously to sweep the shop floor, presenting a vision of industry. This was Richard the errand boy.

On inviting me to Rimmington's on a month's trial in the first instance, Mr Pearlson had added, 'to learn the gentle art of pharmacy'. So here I was ready to be initiated into the gentle art. I was put into Leslie's hands for the introduction. Into my hands was thrust the first piece of essential apparatus. It was not a pestle and mortar, glass measure, not even a stirring rod. It was a duster. Leslie led me into the shop and waved at the shop rounds on the shelves.

> *A nice little job for you, these have all to be dusted two or three times a week, must keep the shop spick and span. I've dusted the blessed things for three years, I'm glad to get rid of that job!*

There was a light ladder in the corner that I could use to reach the top rows. The reason for the brown shop coat now dawned on me. A white coat would have shown the muck in no time, it was bad enough with a brown coat which turned into a dirty grey with layers of dust I moved. The shop was situated on a busy cross-roads and the passing traffic stirred up clouds of dust. Shipley was one of the many West Riding mill towns; a dozen or more mill chimneys rained smoke, soot and grime down on the streets. 'Wheer ther's muk ther's brass' is an old Yorkshire motto. I thought there ought to be a fortune lying about in Rimmington's judging by the amount I shifted.

Mr Dwyer came down into the shop and passed a pleasant word or two and assured me that a junior apprentice's life did not all consist of dusting, there were better things to follow. 'Take note of the names of the drugs as you dust the bottles,' he advised, 'then you can look on dusting as educational.' I might give a wry smile but to me the whole job seemed quite menial. However from then on I always carried a duster in my overall pocket and the habit stuck even when I qualified; a MPS with a duster!

It took me a good hour to dust my bottles. Meanwhile Mr Pearlson our dispenser had arrived. He travelled from Leeds by train and miraculously was nearly always late. The LMS and LNER were evidently as reliable in their day as British Rail would be later. That was Pearlson's tale; Mr Dwyer's opinion was that 'the lazy sod can't get up in a morning.' However now that he had arrived and I'd finished my dusting I was placed in his qualified hands for my initiation into 'The gentle art'.

Show cases on one side of the shop were backed by a mahogany screen. Behind it, hidden from the customers, was the dispensing counter where medicines were concocted. I was to work there under the dispenser's eye. He set me on packing what we called 'packed drugs'. If you buy a packet of Bicarbonate of Soda these days it will come in a greaseproof bag, enclosed in a carton printed with its name, directions for use, warnings, expiry date. Not in 1932 at Rimmington's. Powders had to be weighed out on squares of white paper, which had to be neatly folded, made into a packet either with sealing wax or fine chemist's twine, a label, often handwritten, had to be stuck on. After all that labour a four ounce packet of Bicarb sold for 2 pence. No wonder apprentices were not highly paid. We packed several powders in this way, Flowers of Sulphur, Borax etc. We also packed several liquids like Liquid Paraffin and Olive Oil. I started with none of these. Pearlson directed me to the back room where among an array of jars of ointments I would find one labelled 'Ung Hyd Ox Flav.' - abbreviated Latin for Yellow Oxide of Mercury Ointment, commonly called Golden Eye Ointment. I also had to find a box of little tins which had a picture of an eye on the lid and the name. These were less than an inch across. Quite expertly Mr Pearlson showed me how easy it was to take a dollop of the ointment on the end of a bone spatula, deposit it in the tin and smooth the surface. Not easy for clumsy me. I could get little in the tin and a great deal on the counter and my coat. Leslie, happening to pass remarked that the old-fashioned way was best - inside the tin: I graduated to packing liquids.

Leslie said that we could do with some Cod Liver Oil packing. He had a wicked mind. We bought Cod Liver Oil in Winchesters, bottles holding half a gallon. I was shown how easy it was to hold a Winchester in the palm of your right hand and pour directly into a medicine bottle held in the left. I tried and got Cod Liver Oil on my overall. Next wash day there were complaints at home when the fishy smell was imparted to the family laundry.

I did get round to the gentle art at last. Mixing medicines I had to learn new sets of units. Apothecaries ounces, which had 480 grains as opposed to the 437.5 grains of an 'ordinary' ounce. Then there was the fluid ounce, quite confusing when you'd always thought ounce was just a weight. There were 20 ounces to a pint. An ounce was subdivided into eight drams each of 60 minims. A minim, near enough, was 'a drop'. Your doses of potent liquids, tinctures or whatever, were often given in minims. A fluid dram was translated, for directions, as a teaspoonful; four drams (half an ounce) was one tablespoonful. These were represented on prescriptions by strange hieroglyphics.

An important part of training was the reading of prescriptions. Doctors must have taken courses in bad writing; many were illegible. Customers would say *'I don't know how you can read this?'* We didn't either, guesswork came into it. Fortunately most were straight forward, just a few words. When National Insurance was introduced in the 1920s, the only ones who got free medicines were the employed who had their cards stamped, but the number of prescriptions had increased. To make prescribing easier insurance committees had issued 'Formularies', recipe books which contained formulae for standard treatments. Most important were the mixtures

Figure 5. The author in 1939. *Alex Robinson*

(misturae) for the old bottles of medicine: the physician's standby. Each formula was given a name in Latin. There was *Mist Alba* (White Mixture), *Mist Expectorans* (for bronchitis), *Mist Tussis* (Cough Mixture) and so on. Instead of writing a number of ingredients the doctor just wrote *'Mist* whatever', quantity and dose. The finished bottle, with an old-fashioned cork pressed in (no screw tops) and a handwritten label, had to be wrapped in white paper and closed in sealing wax. No just dropping it in a paper bag as today.

To Other Duties

I was eventualy allowed to serve customers after suitable grooming. Other things to learn now: prices and whereabouts of a range of patent medicines; Holloway's Pills, Grasshopper Ointment, Kurem Ointment; there were strange products called Dr Hooper's Female Pills. This leads me to mention the sale of contraceptives strangely enough. Nowadays we see displays of Durex on shop counters; would you believe that in 1932 they were kept locked up in the safe and supplies were only made by the senior staff! Times change. I think also of many items we sold regularly such as Bronchitis kettles. Someone laid up with bronchial pneumonia had to have an atmosphere laden with warm water vapour. For 'chesty' children we sold pneumonia jackets - basically thick pads of wadding tied round the chest.

In a working class area where money was tight patent medicines were often beyond reach. We made up countless bottles of favourite recipes. Notes would arrive: three pennyworth each of Liquorice, Chlorodyne and Marshmallow. No Benylin for a cold, a few pennorth of Sweet Spirit of Nitre, which made you sweat, was asked for, or perhaps vile tasting Ammoniated Tincture of Quinine. Infants were luckier, they had a wonderful cough mixture, sweet tasting Oil of Almonds and Syrup of Violets and Squills. There was also a concoction for adults called 'All Fours'. The four were oils of Aniseed and Peppermint, Paregoric and Laudanum. Laudanum is Tincture of Opium, only sold diluted. Paregoric also contained Laudanum and was quite potent. 'All Fours' was sold in small quantities and made into a home medicine by adding to a pan of hot water into which black treacle had been poured. Sometimes whole linseed was boiled in the water and strained off. The resulting syrup was very comforting.

People were more self-reliant where health was concerned. No NHS until 1949 and working class folk only called the doctor in as a last resort in serious illnesses. Lots of folk depended on herbal treatments. We sold a range of common herbs in twopenny packets.

Some chemists specialised in so-called 'counter prescribing'. 'Can you make me up a good cough bottle?' was a common cry. The cost of a doctor's visit was reflected in pleas as 'I'm crippled with rheumatics, can you do owt for me?' We always tried, it was a paying game, more profitable than selling patent medicines, and if they wanted further supplies they had to come back to you.

A Change from Medicine

The novelty of getting involved in medicine had just begun to wear off as we got into autumn. Rimmingtons had a wine and spirits licence, much rarer than they are today when every grocer's shop sells booze. Only a few chemists and the occasional high class grocer had an off-licence, temperance societies opposed them strongly. Then there was not the demand, 'ordinary folk' did not drink wine every day, spirits were a luxury only the better off could afford. Only at Christmas did any appreciable demand arise. Most households would have a bottle of cheap port or sherry and, if lucky, a half bottle of whisky or rum. The latter, essential for rum sauce, might be bought in 'noggins' from a pub.

Just as we packed many of our medicinal products so we packed some of our own wines which we bought in casks, laid on a gantry in the wine cellar. We would collect empty wine bottles, giving customers one penny each for any they brought back. Richard had the job of washing them out and leaving them to dry in cases.

One day in November Leslie said we'd better start bottling ready for Christmas. He told me to cart some cases of empty bottles into the cellar, some corks, a jug of warm water to soften them in, and a hairbrush. The latter made a mallet to knock the corks in! We had a barrel of 'Tent Wine'! This was cheap British, red wine, a substitute for port. It sold at half-a-crown a bottle. Then we had a cask of genuine port. We used two different labels on bottles for this. One said it was 'Ruby Port' (which cost four shillings and sixpence), the other said it was 'Fine Old Port' (price five shillings and sixpence!). Interestingly some lady would come in and try the 'Fine Old' and later report how much better it was than the cheaper wine. Marvellous what a label can do! I have memories of other wines sold at Christmas. Tarragon, cheap red wine came in oval quart flagons, favourite for some of the mill 'fuddles'. There was a craze for cheap wine cocktails, sweet wines with fruit flavourings and names like 'Late Night Final', 'Green Goddess', in fancy bottles giving the working class a feeling of the high life.

Christmas was a busy time on the perfumery side. Cheap

perfumes, Californian Poppy, Evening in Paris, June, and many more came in novelty packs - top hats, model animals, plastic Eiffel Towers containing a small bottle for about five shillings. Talcum powders and bath cubes in fancy boxes. For ten shillings you could get something better by firms like Yardley and Coty. It was a busy time, last minute shopping was the rule. On Christmas Eve we would be open until 11 pm. For years I was too tired to enjoy Christmas. Mrs Rimmington gave me a £1 tip for the extra work. Made you feel rich.

Leslie left at Christmas, his apprenticeship ended. Like Mr Dwyer he never qualified but became a commercial traveller, selling chemists' sundries. I took his place as senior (only!) apprentice. I'd learned a lot in four months, polishing dispensing skills and serving customers. I was no longer 'thrown' when asked for strange things. In my first weeks I thought they were pulling my leg when asked for 'Devil's Dung'. Not so, we had such a commodity, an evil-smelling resin. Likewise 'Dragon's Blood', a red powder. Goodness knows what they used them for but we sold them. We sold Yellow Ochre by the pound for colour washing cellar kitchens and a range of resins and oils and washing materials unheard of these days.

My practice at dispensing was helped by an epidemic of flu in January. We had queues after every surgery of folk with prescriptions for colds and rheumatism. A great thing about the apprentice system was that you learned as you worked. Nowadays students go to university for four years then have to learn how to run a shop. Medicine in our day was simpler. No computers, no antibiotics or miracle drugs. Yet I believe the old time chemist had a better, more satisfying life. When you handed over a bottle of mixture, made with your own hands, you were handing over a bit of medical magic. How can a box of tablets with a computer generated label compare?

Life as an apprentice was a hard slog, long hours at work, then three evenings at night school to learn your theory. There were light moments to brighten it. Like the time a clumsy assistant dropped a Winchester of strongest ammonia and cleared the shop with its fumes. One summer day we fermented a gallon of malt extract in the attic, making beer surreptitiously. It over fermented filling a stock room with froth. We had a painful task putting dogs to sleep with prussic acid. One got away leading Richard a merry dance through the town. An irate owner brought the 'ghost' back next day.

I said at the start I did not want to be a chemist. In the event I've stuck it for 60 years and it has not been all that bad, in spite of the long hours and tedious customers. Once that apprenticeship was over and the magic M.P.S, obtained, I've enjoyed being a chemist.

5. ON THE WAY TO THE TOP: JOHN BRAINE'S BRADFORD

by Philip Colehan

'ALL I KNEW WAS THAT I WAS A FAILURE at the age of 35, not even able to provide a home for my wife and the coming child. And the novel on which I had pinned my hopes had been rejected by four publishers.' Such was the state of mind of John Braine in 1956. But in March 1957 *Room at the Top*, the first novel by this Bradford born and bred author, became an instant literary and financial success. From being a nobody he became, almost overnight, a celebrity whom everybody wanted to know. He remained in the public eye until his death in London in October 1986, yet it was the first half of his life spent in Bradford which were crucial formative years, when he watched and observed people and places before re-creating them as fictional characters and settings in his books.

John was born in April 1922 at his grandparent's house.(Figure 1)

My grandmother's house always smelled of wax tapers and roast beef.
It stood at the top of Sedgefield Terrace, a narrow grimy street off

Figure 1. John, left, and cousins outside his grandparents Sedgefield Terrace house. *Mary Tate*

Westgate in Bradford. Opposite the house was St Patrick's Church, built for the first influx of refugees from the Irish famine.

Though I have not lived there since I was a child it is the one place in the world to which I feel I belong. I can remember the district lovingly and in detail at any time, recalling with pleasure its terrace houses with tiny front gardens, its off-licence shops, its post office which sells comic postcards and pictures of the Sacred Heart; the Washington, the Beehive and the Harp of Erin, and even the Council flats off White Abbey.

From Westgate the road ran on past White Abbey towards Heaton which was, and is, termed a better class district. That is a district where people have more money. The better off in England move out of the smoke they have done so much to create, and it is possible to measure a man's income group by the height above sea-level where he lives.

This strong affection for his earliest roots is again clearly reflected in the foreword to his biography of fellow Bradfordian author, J.B.Priestley. He writes of their common background,

I was born in a street less than two miles from the street where he was born, and off the same road. The Bradford in which he grew up was, outwardly at least, the Bradford in which I grew up. The countryside around Bradford was the same. Above all, the moors were the same. It was still a city with a character of its own; not a beautiful city, but a nourishing city, a city to love.

Soon after he was born his parents moved to Harehill Road, Thackley, where he and his sister Mary grew up. His father, Fred, was employed as a superintendent at Bradford Corporation's sewage works at Esholt. Fred came from a Midlands nonconformist family; he had served in the Great War and had a reserved disposition which concealed a well-informed, intelligent mind. Of greater influence upon John was his mother Katherine (née Henry). She had worked at the old Bradford Central Library and came from a family with a strong Irish-Catholic background. Her love of books and reading were transferred to John, as was her devotion to the Roman Catholic Church. By the time he was five he had decided that he would become a writer and nothing else!

It was in the infants' class at Thackley School where I first met John. Years later he wrote of it,

Thackley Board School is a solid, vaguely Gothic building in local stone, with an asphalt playground, ferocious spiked railings and a sizeable playing field. As a child I thought it remarkably handsome,

Figure 2. Thackley Board School building building today. *Bob Duckett*

and I still do. And I never thought it depressing. (Figure 2)

We were both Roman Catholics and although I knew that in some sense we were different to other boys and girls, for me it had no effect upon relationships with other children. Not so to John. Already he had an obviously different, independent streak of mind which singled him out, and for which he was occasionally ragged and bullied. Of this period he claimed, 'Being in a minority is extremely valuable. One is pitchforked into the only tenable position for a writer; on the outside looking in.'

On the whole he enjoyed a happy childhood for in those days Thackley was much less built up than it is today. For children there was plenty of opportunity for adventure, roaming in Buck Wood, Ella Carr and Mally Hutton fields. John joined his friends in climbing trees, making dens, lighting fires, and even swimming in the Leeds and Liverpool canal. He also made good use of the Idle branch of Bradford Public Libraries. It was housed in a fine building which had

Figure 3. The building that was Idle Library. John's sister worked here. *Bob Duckett*

previously served as local council offices. (Figure 3) One corner of the ground floor lending library was reserved as a children's section from which we were allowed to borrow only one fiction and one non-fiction book at a time. John was already a voracious and rapid reader and so his mother was often called upon to change library books on his behalf. It was her guidance and good taste which helped to develop his appreciation of good literature.

John's father, who was a keen sportsman, was less successful in encouraging him to play cricket or football. He had no natural aptitude for ball games and even less interest. One of his father's hobbies which did have an impact on the family was that of entering competitions in newspapers and magazines. He won various modest prizes before winning about £700 in 1933. On the strength of this they moved to a detached house with a large garden at 720 Leeds Road, Thackley. (Figure 4)

In 1933 John and I won scholarships to St Bede's Grammar School, Heaton, and had our names inscribed in gold lettering on the

Figure 4. John Braine's mother on the doorstep of the family's Thackley house. *Mary Tate*

Honours Board at Thackley School. To travel from Thackley to Heaton meant taking two tram rides and this in itself was an adventure. As he wrote,

> *There aren't any trams in Bradford now, more's the pity; but at that time they were still running on some routes, and all had the splendid*

feature of an open portion with wooden seats. Whatever the weather we always rode in the open; the enclosed part was for the soft unadventurous grown ups. Riding perched high in the open with the wind and the rain in your face you were really travelling, not simply going from one place to another. And the quietest boy used to feel a little drunk and rowdy with speed and fresh air; you wanted to shout and sing and show everyone what a fine fellow you were.

Although on most days we travelled to school by tram, we walked part of the way home in order to save the tram fare; the penny saved was enough to buy us a bag full of sweets. Our route took us by Heaton parish church, through a snicket between houses, down onto Frizinghall Road and into Shipley where we caught the tram for the last leg of the journey to Thackley. On these daily walks we invented a surreal story which we elaborated and developed bit by bit. In some

Figure 5. John, right, with colleagues at Bradford Technical College. *Mary Tate*

of the mean streets off Canal Road we fantasized about a gang of evil people ruled over by an obscenely fat old woman, Nellie. The gang was called the Vodi, and if some hapless person fell foul of Nellie then they were sure to suffer. Years after we had invented these fantasies John remembered and used them, first in a magazine article and then in 1959 in a full length novel called *The Vodi*.

Academically he was not a success at St Bede's, leaving in 1938 without a School Certificate. He did not blame St Bede's and said, 'It was certainly not due to any shortcomings of the staff that I wasted my time there. Initially it was the size of the school which overwhelmed me, an experience with which I didn't have the moral fibre to cope.' In an open letter to the sixth form in 1958 he concluded, 'Make the most of your chances now; they will not come again, and you may not be as tough or as fortunate as I.'

Jobs were not easy to come by in Bradford in the late 1930s and the only job that he could get when he left school was that of a laboratory assistant at Bradford Technical College. (Figure 5) 'There may have been a laboratory assistant who was more idle, who broke more expensive glassware and equipment, one who was less fitted for the world of science, but I have yet to hear of him.' So that job didn't last long. For a time he was an assistant in Pratt's furniture shop and then a progress chaser at Hepworth and Grandage's. But his most satisfying job was in Mickey White's second hand bookshop in a basement under shops in Westgate. Mickey was an eccentric character who, for example, always wore a bowler hat with a drawing pin through the brim so he could stick it onto the wall anywhere he wanted. In summertime he went about barefoot and would set off on prolonged hiking trips as the fancy took him. John was in his element, virtually his own boss, a cellarfull of books to read, gossiping about literature with the few customers who braved the steep staircase and the Stygian gloom. At the end of the day he would emerge, blinking in the daylight like a troglodyte.

He spent most of his free time studying, reading and writing stories and poems. He also discovered the existence of girls. There were then not many opportunities to mix, so on Sunday evenings boys and girls would gather on what became known as 'monkey parades' or 'bunny runs'. John said if you don't know what they are you haven't lived, and went on,

That's another snapshot; a November night on the moors, the yellow street lamps on the roads through the town and the blackness beyond, where boys and girls passed and re-passed, always in pairs, eventually

Figure 6. The Bingley Library building 1976 in which John Braine worked. *Bradford Libraries*

after as long as two hours plucking up courage, making away arm-in-arm to the benches at the side of the road. The girls never lost sight of each other and it was all quite innocent.

Then came the war, and with it the end of the monkey parades and the closure of the bookshop. Fortuitously for John a job became vacant at Bingley Public Library for which he applied and was appointed. The job suited him, he was knowledgeable about books, and he liked Bingley and the people he met there. (Figure 6) In June 1942 he was drafted into the Royal Navy and trained as a wireless telegraphist, but before going on active service he was found to be suffering from tuberculosis and sent to Grassington Sanatorium (which was the hospital for patients from Bradford suffering from TB). At that time this lung disease often proved fatal and treatment was fresh air, nourishing food and rest. John used this enforced rest to good effect. He applied himself to writing and produced a poem a day throughout his stay in hopital. One of them was published in a small magazine and whilst he received no payment, he 'didn't care, I was a writer and that was all that mattered.' He also studied for the School Certificate which he passed in the summer of 1944. By then he had been discharged from Grassington and was back working at Bingley Public Library.

When I was demobilized from the RAF we decided together to attend Leeds School of Librarianship in 1947-48, following which we became Chartered librarians. He returned to Bingley as Senior Assistant Librarian and immersed himself in the social life around

Figure 7. John Braine, left, and neighbour Kenneth in 1943. *Mary Tate*

the Little Theatre.(Figure 8) A verse play *Desert in the Mirror* which he had written received its first (and only) production in Bingley Little Theatre in July 1950. It was based upon the theme of Faust, the man who sells his soul for wealth and then wishes he hadn't. 'On its second night the play attracted an audience of about a dozen, six of whom left half way through' commented John. Nevertheless it attracted encouraging attention from some critics and was to give him an idea for a future novel.

His father gave him the push he needed. 'Why on earth', he asked John, 'don't you write an article on something you know about?' He knew something about Little Theatres and so,

> I wrote an article about the kind of pub patronised by members of the Little Theatre. It was fictional in approach but was based solidly on fact; it was accepted by Tribune immediately. There was no letter of

Figure 8. The Bingley Little Theatre 1948 production of *Saloon Bar*. John Braine, in cap and muffler, is second from the left. *G. Tillet and Mary Tate*

> *acceptance, the Literary Editor simply sent me the galley proofs to correct. I realised I had crossed the bridge which divides the amateur from the professional. This may appear naive, but anyone who has collected 200 rejection slips, as I had done, will understand.*

On the strength of this, and several other acceptances, he pondered about his future.

> *I needed to meet people, to read, to go to the theatre and cinema, and, most important of all, I needed to walk around the city streets and sit in cafes and pubs watching and listening. It wasn't possible to do all those things and work, so in 1951 I resigned my job and went to London to be a full time writer...it was the most stupid thing I ever did. But from then on I was in control of my own life. It was like the difference between being in prison and being in battle. You may be killed in battle, it's true; but you might as well be killed as live in prison.*

And nearly kill himself he did, living in poverty in a cheap Kensington bed-sit. In eight months he earned £100 as a writer. Then in November 1951 his mother was knocked down and killed in a road accident only a few yards from her home in Leeds Road, Thackley. When he came home for the funeral he looked desperately ill, and within a few weeks he was diagnosed as having a recurrence of tuberculosis. He was admitted to Grassington Sanatorium again and remained there for eighteen months.(Figure 9)

> *There was no loneliness at Grassington. And there was time to read and write and to talk and think. It was here in the autumn of 1952 that I began to write 'Room at the Top'; partly I think to prove to myself that I was only wounded and not defeated...if you don't board your destiny at the time its scheduled to stop for you, the guard won't back it up for you, and it will never stop for you again.*

When he was discharged from hospital he went to stay with his father and sister who were now living on Park Road, Thackley. Whilst convalescing he finished off the final draft of his novel which he first titled *Born Favourite*, then changed it to *Joe for King*, before eventually settling for *Room at the Top*. Whilst his agent tried to obtain a publisher John decided to return to librarianship. Despite having expressed the view that, 'Being a writer in a library is a bit like being a eunuch in a harem', he obtained a post as Branch Librarian at Newbiggin with the Northumberland County Library Service. Living in digs there he met and fell in love with with an attractive young school teacher, Pat Wood. In October 1955 they married, and

Figure 9. John Braine in his wartime sanatorium study-cum-bedroom at Grassington. *Mary Tate*

shortly afterwards moved to Wakefield on his appointment as Branch Librarian at Darton. His pay was £12 a week.

Many years later he wrote about his feelings at this stage of his life. His novel had just been accepted for publication and Pat was expecting their first child. They came home to stay with his father for Christmas 1956.

> *What I missed in Wakefield was what I had been brought up with in Thackley, instant access to the moors. I can't do without unspoilt countryside.... In the evening we walked down to the George in Leeds Road, Idle, where the landlord and his family were friends. A group of us walked home, it was a clear and frosty night with the moon riding high and we called at a friend's house for a goodnight drink. Pat and I went home to a supper of strong tea, cold beef and pickled onions. We awoke to a view of Buck Woods - all that we had was love and hope in the future. Yes, that was the best Christmas of my life.*

Some weeks later my wife and I were visiting John and Pat in Wakefield. It was a Sunday and John and I went out for a lunchtime pint. *Room at the Top* had been published that week and it received glowing reviews in all the Sunday newspapers. So I asked John what amount of money he hoped to make from the book. He said that if he made enough to provide a staircarpet and a wardrobe for the bedroom he would be satisfied. Within a matter of weeks the book became an outstanding bestseller and the money began to roll in. He resigned his job and bought a fine house in Park Road, Bingley - a road which leads up on to the moors. His childhood dream had come true and he was making his way to the top. (Figure 10)

> Note. Quotations in the text are taken from the author's collection of cuttings from newspapers and magazine articles.

Figure 10. John Braine, 1957. *Philip Cole*

6. Burned To The Ground: Fires in Bradford's History

by David J Croft

WHILST LOCAL HISTORIANS UP AND DOWN THE LAND
are diligently striving to preserve and record as much of the past as
they can, they are often forced to face up to a formidable adversary
- fire. Fire, possibly more than any other disaster is no respecter of
persons, and both amateur and professional historians sometimes
have to contend with its effects. I am sure that at some time or
another we have all seen a favourite shop, church or industrial
building burned to the ground, and whilst loss of life may not have
occurred, the community around it may have suffered a significant
loss. The mill towns of the north of England have possibly suffered
more from fire than many others with the possible exception of

Figure 1. Horse-drawn fire engine on Westgate Hill, c.1905. *Bradford Libraries*

places such as Coventry, Hull and Plymouth which were devastated during the Second World War.

Records show that the first fire appliance appeared in Bradford in 1806 when three horse-drawn engines arrived. The appliances came under the control of the new local authority in 1847, and the horse-drawn engines remained in use until 1914, being supplemented by steam-powered vehicles from 1867 and petrol-driven ones from 1908. (Figure 1) The efficiency of the early fire engines was severely limited by the hilly terrain of the city and the pulling power of the horses. Buildings were often razed to the ground before the brigade could get to the scene of a fire. This was the case at the fire at Manningham Mills in 1871 when the horses failed to climb Westgate. However, the increased power of later motorised appliances was also matched by larger fires at larger buildings which frequently necessitated the summoning of additional fire-fighting resources from neighbouring towns.

Over the past hundred years or so, Bradford has witnessed many conflagrations, both large and small which have resulted in the destruction of many well-known landmarks. Probably the greatest number of fires in the city during this period has, not surprisingly occurred in places associated with the textile industry. The combination of wool products, greasy floors, and no doubt the occasional carelessly discarded match or cigarette has wreaked havoc with the city's chief industry and employer.(Figure 2)

Figure 2. Passengers arriving at the refurbished Forster Square rail station below, get a stark reminder of Bradford's past, and the destructive power of fire. *Bob Duckett*

It is ironic that the city's first worsted mill should have suffered in this way, for had it survived, the Holme Mill would no doubt have been a major industrial attraction in the city. Built in 1800 by a partnership of Ramsbotham, Swaine and Murgatroyd, the premises survived barely four years before being almost destroyed by fire in March 1804. The ruins were subsequently purchased by Richard Fawcett of Great Horton and rebuilt.

The city's largest mill complex, Lister's in Manningham, has probably suffered more than most, for it has been affected by no less than five major fires. The first, in February 1871, completely destroyed the original mill which had been built in 1838. Within two years the new mill, which remains with us today, dominating the city skyline, had been opened. Designed by architects Andrews & Pepper, the new mill occupied an area of eighteen acres, and at one time employed five thousand people in its vast weaving sheds.

It is fortunate that the four subsequent fires at Manningham Mills affected buildings away from the main mill complex. The second blaze, on Sunday 23 June 1889, was in a separate building close to Beamsley Road which sadly resulted in the deaths of two firemen. Three workers lost their lives in the fire on 15 April 1913 when a separate shed at the Scotchman Road end of the site was destroyed. A two-storey laboratory used by the dyeing department was gutted in a blaze on 28 December 1919, this again being a separate building close to Beamsley Road. Wartime secrecy prevented the detailed reporting of the blaze on 1 June 1941 which the Telegraph & Argus merely reported as 'at a Bradford building'. On this occasion, a single-storey building was destroyed causing several thousands of pounds worth of damage.

Looking back over the years it is interesting to see how the major fires in textile premises can be grouped into particular geographical areas - notably Little Germany, the Leeds Road area, and the Union Street/Nelson Street area. The area known today as Little Germany was largely developed in the period between 1860 and 1874, and consisted entirely of warehouses and related offices. It is therefore not surprising that over the last century a number of the buildings in this unique area have been damaged or destroyed by fire.

The premises at 4 Currer Street had been built in 1859 by Lockwood & Mawson, and were purchased by the firm of Downs, Coulter & Co Ltd in 1917, and were used by them until 1976. For a number of years the premises were used for wool storage, until the top story was damaged by fire in March 1986. After two years of neglect the building was re-roofed and restored, only to be destroyed by another fire in August 1990.

The site of Festival Square was once a warehouse known as 19, Peckover Street. Built around 1858, the building was last used by a firm of paper merchants, but was destroyed by fire in the mid-1970s and was finally demolished in 1979.

Just beyond Little Germany, the area around Leeds Road/Hammerton Street/Edderthorpe Street has also witnessed much damage. In the space of an hour and a half on the evening of Saturday 7 June 1913, an arsonist struck at three separate firms causing severe damage, and minor damage to a number of other premises in the area. A similar spate of fires had occurred during 1907 resulting in serious damage to the Mount Street spinning mills and at premises in Edderthorpe Street itself.

Across the city centre in the Union Street/Nelson Street area, numerous blazes altered the landscape, especially during the 1930s. The area itself was largely developed between 1875 and 1898 and was dominated by the Union Warehouse of 1876. A further blaze in

Figure 3. Bradford Fire Brigade engines, and admirers, at the Central Fire Station, Nelson Street, 1922. *Eye Ubiquitous and Dorothy Burrows*

Union Street in 1963 caused more property to be demolished.

These isolated fires were of relatively little consequence compared with the conflagration which occurred on 3 June 1965. In what was described at the time as the city's worst fire in peace-time, and possibly this century, a large tract of warehouses in Nelson Street, Crossland Street, Arundel Street and Croft Street were the scene of a massive daytime blaze which could be seen for miles around, and caused over a million pound's worth of damage. The site is today occupied by the Jacob's Well car park. Further up Nelson Street, the Britannia Mills complex was badly damaged in June 1991, resulting in demolition.

Of course it was not just city centre premises which were razed to the ground. A spectacular blaze at the Cliffe Mills premises of William Ramsden & Co Ltd in Bartle Lane, Great Horton in October 1919 completely wiped out the eleven acre complex which had a circumference of over a mile. Thousands of onlookers watched as firemen from Keighley and Leeds narrowly prevented terraced houses in Great Horton Road from being engulfed in the inferno. Across town, the Union Mills at Eccleshill were gutted in July 1905, and at Greengates, the Albion Mills were similarly destroyed six years later.

It is said that lightning rarely strikes twice in the same place, but fire sometimes does. As we have seen earlier, some businesses have suffered several major fires at the same site. Charles Semon, a leading member of the city's German community had warehouse premises in Church Bank on the edge of the Little Germany area. These burned down in 1877 and were replaced by new premises not far away in Bolton Road.

Designed by the notable firm of Milnes & France, they too succumbed to fire in the 1920s.

An even rarer example of fire striking twice involved the triangular plot of buildings bounded by Forster Square, Canal Road and Commercial Street. This conglomeration of warehouses and offices was the scene of a massive blaze in November 1896. It was reported at the time that the fire brigade had been hampered by a lack of appliances as a new one which was being built for the Corporation had itself been destroyed by fire at the works of its makers in London! Eventually, the private fire engine belonging to W& J.Whitehead at Laisterdyke was summoned, though even this was unable to prevent the site from near total destruction. Fifty-four years later in June 1950, the premises built on the site of the 1896 blaze were themselves the scene of a spectacular fire which caused almost a quarter of a million pound's worth of damage. This time, re-building did not take place, and in 1959 a row of single-storey shops was built on part of the site.

Such large fires as these brought thousands of eager sightseers to the scene which frequently caused problems of crowd-control for the police. At the massive fire in Palmerston Buildings, Manor Row, in September 1913, police had difficulty keeping the spectators under control, and women fainted in the crush and had to be carried away.

Entertainment

Places of entertainment where large numbers of people gathered were obviously prone to fire. Cinemas in particular were vulnerable, with many of the audience smoking, and all occupying upholstered seats. The dangers were not confined to the auditorium either, for upstairs projection boxes with over-heated projection equipment and reels of film were between them recipes for disaster. The year 1940 saw the peak in cinema-going in the city when no fewer than forty-two picture houses were in business in Bradford. Many of these succumbed to minor fires, such as The Rialto, Clayton (1953), The Coronet, Undercliffe (1955), and the Victoria Picture Palace, Girlington (1955), but were re-opened after short periods of closure for re-building.

Some of the city's larger cinemas met a fiery end altogether. The Empire Theatre and Opera House in Great Horton Road had opened in August 1916, but was destroyed by fire a little over a year later. The premises were rebuilt and re-opened as a cinema in 1918 and lasted until 1952 before being burnt down again, resulting in demolition.

The New Tatler at the end of Thornton Road, close to Town Hall Square had an interesting history. Opening in time for Christmas 1912, it had been converted from a warehouse, and through several changes of name became the New Tatler in 1935. A fire in December 1945 resulted in its demolition, and the site was re-developed incorporating Walden's bedding store.

Several city cinemas closed with the decline in cinema-going in the 1960's, but later re-opened showing Asian films; The Essoldo in Manningham Lane was a good example. It closed in October 1965 and saw use as an Asian cinema between 1968 and 1976 before a fire ended its days.

The Towers Hall in Manchester Road met a similar fate in 1970. The Elite in Toller Lane was destroyed in a blaze in 1988, a local radio station mis-pronouncing the name as the Alight Cinema. It truly was!

The Prince's Theatre in Little Horton Lane is thought to have been unique in Britain in having one theatre built on top of another. The Prince's opened in April 1876 above the Star Music Hall which had opened the previous year. On Tuesday 16 July, a small fire broke out in the building. A passer-by noticed the blaze and ran to the Town Hall to inform the police. For some reason they were unable to sound the fire alarm, and a policeman had to run to the fire station to summon the brigade! Whilst all these delays were taking place, the fire was gaining a hold on the building, and by the time the brigade were on the scene they were too late to save the Prince's which was totally destroyed. Gossip at the time called it 'divine retribution' as the two places of entertainment had been built on the site of the former St John's Church!

Roller skating was a popular pastime in late-Victorian and Edwardian times, and Bradford had a number of such venues. The first craze for skating developed in the 1870s and 1880s, but soon died out, only to be revived again in the early 1900s. In this second phase, four skating rinks were established in the city - the first being the Rolarena in Manningham Lane which opened in November 1908. This was followed by the Coliseum in Toller Lane, the Hippodrome in Barkerend Road, and the Towers Hall in Manchester Road. One by one they all closed, leaving the Rolarena as the last skating rink in the city. Whilst it was closed for alterations in July 1955, a fire broke out in the basement, and within forty minutes the building was no more. The Rolarena's demise also saw the end of this popular craze, and in 1960 the Mecca Ballroom (now Maestro's) was built on the site offering more sophisticated entertainment.

Two other notable city centre public buildings to have been affected by fire are Textile Hall in Westgate and Eastbrook Hall in Leeds Road. Textile Hall opened in March 1915 to house the many local textile trades unions. With the decline of the textile industry it was largely vacated by 1980, and in August the following year, fire swept through the top floor, and the building was subsequently rebuilt as a two-storey building with a flat roof. Eastbrook Hall was a popular meeting place which had opened in March 1904. Once again, by the 1980s it was little used, but fire severely damaged the building in February 1996, and its future is uncertain.

Not far away, the Bradford Playhouse in Chapel Street has been a particularly unlucky building. Originally known as Jowett Hall, it was badly damaged by fire in March 1935, and re-opened as the Civic Playhouse in January 1937. July 1996 saw it destroyed again, re-opening as The Priestley Centre for the Arts in November 1997.

Schools

No doubt many school-children over the years have wished that their school would burn down, freeing them from boring lessons, and a good number of children have been so rewarded, though mostly in recent years. An earlier school fire was that at the Carlton High School for Boys in Carlton Street, Great Horton Road, in November 1949. Whilst the pupils had their wishes granted, they were soon re-housed in the empty premises of the Bradford Grammer School in Manor Row, the former occupants having moved out to their new premises in Keighley Road in 1945. However, this was not quite the end of the story, for although Carlton later moved out to new premises in Undercliffe Lane, the Manor Row buildings were engulfed in flames in May 1987 whilst in the ownership of Amrik Electronics who had planned to the use the building for making satellite television equipment.

A spate of school fires in the last thirty years or so has seen the destruction or partial destruction of Undercliffe Junior High School (1966), St Patrick's Girls' School (also 1966) and Allerton Junior School (1968). In more recent times, the same weekend in November 1990 saw arson attacks at both Gregory Middle School in Rooley Lane and Tyersal First School in Fearnville Drive, resulting in the children being moved to other accommodation.

Churches

The fact that churches and chapels have fared better with regard to fire has probably little to do with divine intervention but more with the construction of the buildings and their clientele. Solid stone buildings containing little wood or fabric are less vulnerable to destruction, and the fact that worshippers were not permitted to smoke must have contributed greatly to the survival of most of the city's places of worship. However, this is not to say that all have survived intact. The Great Horton area can claim two such spectacular blazes. The first, in February 1905, totally destroyed the Sunday Schools of the Great Horton Wesleyan Chapel in Paternoster Lane, close to Great Horton Road. A few hundred yards away, the Church of St John the Evangelist in Westcroft Road, was the scene of a big blaze in February 1956. Built in 1874, St John's is a notable landmark, but within an hour, fire had reduced it to a roofless, blackened shell. Re-building work was soon under way, and the west window was re-designed.

The Sunday Schools belonging to the Hallfield Baptist Church, off Manningham Lane, were burnt down on 23 March 1929, but were rebuilt and re-opened within a year on 22 March 1930 with much celebration.

Shops

Considering the size of the city there have been few major shop fires. A particularly spectacular blaze in July 1914 totally destroyed the premises of Carter & Harrisons, a firm of milliners and fancy drapers in Rawson Place. The four-storey premises were struck by lightning during a severe storm, and burned to the ground. The adjoining premises were occupied by the Corporation Gas Stove Department whose manager lived upstairs above the shop. At the time of the fire, the manager's wife was ill in bed and had to be carried out into the

Figure 4. The destruction of Busby's (Debenham's) on Manningham Lane, 1979. *Dorothy Burrows*

Figure 5. Aftermath of Busby's fire.
Dorothy Burrows

street as a precaution, though the fire did not spread in that direction. However, on the other side, Henry Smith's umbrella and walking stick manufacturing business was damaged. The blaze might not have been so severe had an attending fire engine not hit a lamp post in Sunbridge Road throwing a fireman to the ground, and was unable to proceed to the outbreak. The premises in Rawson Place were rebuilt in due course though to a completely different architectural style which can be easily detected to this day.

During the Second World War parts of Rawson Market just across the road from Rawson Place were destroyed during a bombing raid, as were the premises of the well-known firm of Lingard's whose extensive premises in Godwin Street were reduced to ruins in May 1941.

Nearby John Street Market was totally destroyed in a huge blaze on 5 November 1977 (an appropriate date) but none of these could compete with an event which many Bradfordians will never forget - the destruction of Busby's (Debenhams) on Manningham Lane in August 1979. (Figure 4)

At around tea-time on Wednesday 29 August, passers-by noticed smoke coming from upper storey windows of the building which had been empty since the store closed the previous year. Within a short time the entire building was alight from end to end, and fire-fighters were called out from across West Yorkshire to deal with the blaze. Three hours later the city's most famous store which had opened on the site at Easter 1930 was a mass of rubble and twisted metal. (Figure 5) Although arson was suspected, it was never proved, but

Figure 6. Memorial to the Valley Parade (Bradford City Football Club stadium) fire disaster of 1985. *Bob Duckett*

whatever the cause it could certainly claim to be a memorable occasion for the many thousands of people who came to witness what might, apart from the tragic events at Valley Parade in May 1985, be described as Bradford's last great fire. (Figure 6)

7. From Parcel Lad to Leylands: Trolleybus Tales

by Frank Long

AT EASTER IN 1939 I got a job as a Parcel Lad working for the Bradford Corporation Passenger Transport Department. This was considered to be a really good job with good career prospects. Textiles was the main industry in Bradford at that time, but it was in decline with lots of people on short time. My father drove trolleybuses and trams, and had been a parcel lad, conductor and driver before me. I recall a story he told me about something that happened to him in the early twenties. He was driving on the Allerton run and at the Allerton terminus a man asked him if he could turn the bus round the turning circle as he fancied being a driver. Dad said 'No' and left to go and pay a call at the toilets opposite. He then heard the bus start moving and rushed out to see the bus driven round the circle and hitting a pole, pulling the wires down and damaging the bus. Dad got the sack and my mother and grandma went to see the Transport Manager to plead for his job back. There was no 'Lloyd George' (dole) in those days. Dad was taken back on as a 32 hour worker, and worked his way up to 48 hours over the years.

I was fourteen in 1939 and left school that Easter, starting work as a parcel lad. This was only a temporary job in the summer when a lot of drivers and conductors took their annual holidays. Older parcel lads, those over eighteen, took on their jobs for that period, and we youngsters took their place in the Parcels Department. Our wages were ten bob [50p] a week plus a 1/6 [7.5p] a month bonus for good behaviour. Good service was rewarded the year after by being recalled to the job and given a regular post.

We delivered parcels all over Bradford and there was an agreement with other towns to send parcels for them to deliver. (Figure 2) I remember the charges for delivering in the Bradford area were 3d. for a 7lb. parcel, 4d. for 14lbs. and 6d. for 28 lbs. People left parcels at local depots, mainly tram or trolleybus depots, though we had depots in some shops. These parcels were taken to a central office at the bottom of Bolton Road, sorted, and sent out to depots nearest the destination. To get them to a depot like Duckworth Lane we took the

Figure 1. A tight turning circle. *Dorothy Burrows*

Figure 2. Advertisement, 1938-39.
Bradford Libraries

The advertisement reads:

BRADFORD CORPORATION PASSENGER TRANSPORT

PARCEL DEPARTMENT

In addition to the ordinary business
of
COLLECTION AND DELIVERY OF PARCELS
the Department undertakes a

Cash on Delivery Service

the charge for which is reasonable
and the service good. Another feature
is the **distribution of circulars and
bills** by messengers in uniform,
under supervision, a method which
is undoubtedly the best of its kind
for this particular form of advertising.

You will be surprised how much the
Parcel Department can help you.
Just send your requirements to the
Superintendent.

11 FORSTER SQUARE
BRADFORD
C. R. TATTAM, M.Inst.T., A.M.I.E.E.
General Manager.
TELEPHONE 10505.

---

parcels on a hand cart and put them on the trolleybus. The conductors took them off at the relevant depot. One lad, head down, failed to stop his cart at the end of Thornton Road and charged straight into a telephone box window. On reporting this incident he demonstrated what had happened to the Travel Inspector by charging along with his head down, and went straight into the next window!

Another job the Parcel Department undertook was the delivery of school dinners. We collected these from the Green Lane central kitchens. There were big and small canisters containing potatoes, vegetables, custard, meat pies etc. The main tool of our trade on this duty was a dessert spoon in the top pocket. During the ride around from school to school, the driver's mate would be in the back of the van, working hard with the spoon on the food, a dip in the potatoes, a good lick of the spoon, and onto the peas or beans, then another good lick, and a drop of custard or rice pudding. We certanly didn't go hungry. Humping those heavy cans up school steps was hard work though, and there would be left many a trail of gravy, baked beans and custard!

We delivered bottles of medicine. In those days high class doctors had wealthy patients all over the city. The medicines were in glass bottles and packed in well padded cardboard boxes. The delivery charge was 1 1/2d a bottle. Deliveries were often in the late afternoon, and since we were not paid overtime, it was not a popular job. Some people had been having these deliveries for years and whenever a patient 'popped their clogs' (died) the parcel lads used to cheer. That was one less journey to do.

Another job was delivering the *Bradford Gazette*. This was a free weekly paper. It was alright delivering to back-to-backs or terrace houses up Otley Road, but it was a rotten job delivering in the hilly

Figure 3. Bradford City Transport parcels van CKY 871. *Bradford Libraries*

areas of Baildon or to the big houses in Heaton. We lads used a number of dodges to make our life easier. One was to sell to a friendly fish shop owner, or to put two or three copies into every letter box to get through the job quickly (still done today!). Another was to chuck bundles into the canal. This was OK until the string rotted and the canal got clogged with copies of the *Bradford Gazette*. Or one could sneak in and do someone else's, easier, round, like the back-to-backs up the Manchester Road.

We even delivered joints of meat. These were wrapped in brown paper with a label on it with the person's name. My father, who was once a parcel lad at Wyke, remembered delivering milk on the trams. This was carried in a bucket-style can with a lid and hooks for two ladles, one for the pint measure and the other for the half-pint.

It was a good life. I was set on as a temporary parcel lad, but on the outbreak of war the Corporation took us on again because many of the regular staff were called up to fight. Joe Haigh, the Parcel Superintendent, sent for me. After telling me to get my hair cut he offered me a job 'upstairs'. This was where the admin offices were and a big promotion. 'What do you think?' he said.

'No, sir.'

'Why not, boy?'

'Because I'd rather stay with the lads, sir.'

'Get out!' he shouted.

My father was driving on the Saltaire via Thackley route so I waited at the Bolton shed and told him about the interview. 'Get back!' he said, 'and say you'll do it.' I did, but I'd missed my opportunity.

'I'll have a go at that job, sir.'

'Who said so?'

'My Dad.'

'Too late, boy. Get out!'

We got up to all sorts of silly things. When we had done our deliveries and were riding back down into Bradford, we'd say to the drivers 'Let's have a go!' And often they did. I remember once driving a parcel van down St Enoch's Road in Wibsey at great speed. Me!, a seventeen year old lad with no licence! You have to remember, of course, that there was very little traffic in those days. You rarely saw a car.

The Parcels Department was closed in 1949. It was said that Bradford applied for a licence to deliver in other areas, and it was found that they had no licence to deliver anywhere! But it was the time of nationalisation and everything was changing. This was a shame. I think it a pity to see all these private companies delivering goods which the Corporation could have done.

In 1943 I was eighteen and was called up for war service and spent four years in the RAF. During this period the Corporation paid me one pound a week which my mother put in the bank for me. The £200 'nest egg' was very nice!

On returning to the Corporation on demobilisation in 1947 I was sent to train as a conductor. (Figure 4) I was issued with a new uniform, cash bag, and a strap with a metal plate on to which we attached the ticket punch. The ticket racks could be

Figure 4. Frank's first day back at work after demobilisation from the RAF in 1947. *F.Long*

either wood or metal. We preferred metal as you could tap the fingers of the ill-behaved kids and late night drunks, especially on Saturday nights. We used to go down Park Avenue with the Training Inspector who would do an emergency tram stop shouting 'The driver's collapsed. Stop the tram!' We had to knock the power off, put sand down, and then apply the hand brake (winding the brass handle) as fast as possible.

Later I applied to be a driver, and being an old employee, got priority in a trolleybus school. This was after being offered a tram school position, which I refused. The thought of not being able to alter course if anyone was in my way fightened me to death. We learnt to drive mainly up Thornton Road as far as Bell Dean Road, where we reversed round the island just past the bottom of Rhodesway. We had to pass a test including a reverse round Bell Dean. (Figure 5) My test started with a disaster. The chap before

Figure 5. A trolleybus used by the Driver Training School cautiously negotiates the island at the junction of Thornton Road and Bell Dean Road. *J.S.King*

me had been given a signal to stop at a bus stop and he drew right up to a parked car. On being given the bell to go he could not go forward so had to reverse under supervision, so he failed his test. I was told to take over the bus. I set off, only to move backwards! I never thought of the previous driver leaving the control in reverse. Fortunately the inspector let me carry on and I was given a pass certificate.

You then had to do what was called 'permitting'. This is to go on every route with a regular driver to teach you all about the road problems and wiring complications. After filling in my permit sheet I had to have another test on a service bus on Manningham Lane with the inspector as a passenger. At Frizinghall he tapped on the cab window and said he had seen eough to pass me.

At first you became a 'spare' and you went out wherever you were sent, but I applied to become a regular driver so I could work at the Bolton Deport, near were I lived, with three regular routes to Eccleshill, Greengates via Idle, and Saltaire via Thackley. Living in Eccleshill it was easy to cycle in for a 5 am start, or back from a midnight finish. Getting to remote depots meant getting a staff bus in the early morning at 4 am and waiting around until it was time to start. We took a different shift every week, earlies, lates, splits, and show-ups (taking the duties of drivers who were late or sick).

On buses today you have doors and heating. Not so in the 1940s. Entry was at the back of the bus, with no doors and no heating, either in the bus itself or in the separate driver's cab. The order of a winter's day was long-johns, two vests, two pullovers, a very heavy greatcoat, thick driving gloves and fur-lined boots. A small heater was tried in the 1950s but it was pretty useless.

Once you became a regular driver you got a regular conductor and got to work as a team. The ambition of all bus crews was to drive as fast as possible. The more you caught up with the bus in front, the less work there was to do. The driver was to drive as fast as he could of course, often not stopping for waiting passengers. These would be left for the next bus and would make life easier for your conductor. But the conductor had to be fast as well. He would ring the bell quickly, often before the passengers had got on! In those days on Bolton Road we had a fifteen minute service to each destination off peak, and a seven and a half minute service at peak time. The busiest route in Bradford was the Duckworth Lane with an off peak five minute service and a bus every two and a half minutes at peak times, and always full.

I'm afraid my reputation for fast driving went before me. One of

Figure 6. My regular conductor, Nelson Harrison, at the Greengates terminus. *F. Long*

Figure 7. 'The Narrows'. A Saltaire-bound No.40 sets out along Lower Bolton Road, a site now crossed by the Shipley-Airedale Road. *J.S.King*

the friends of my wife used to step back when she saw I was driving and waited for the next bus saying 'I'm not riding with that mad B—–!'

One summer Saturday morning I was driving down what was known as The Narrows (from Wapping Road down Bolton Road into the City centre) and saw a trolleybus in front of me. (Figure 7) I had the silly thought that I would pass him before we got to Bradford. Impossible of course, we were both driving trolleys! You often wonder what you would do in an emergency and I was really pleased with my reactions in the following incident. It was a hot sunny morning and I was sat with both feet on the dashboard doing about 35 mph. The overhead wires were hanging loose having stretched with the heat. I decided to apply the footbrake to slow down. (On a trolleybus the footbrake works first by using power from the overhead wiring, and then by slowing the motor. Further pressure operates air brakes which cause the brake shoes to press on the wheel drums.) I pressed the pedal and nothing happened. I thought 'My God, no brakes!' Then I thought, 'Well, if I cannot stop, instead of going into Bradford at 30 mph on a busy Saturday lunchtime, I had better turn up Stott Hill towards the Cathedral, for up this road there was a warehouse wall. If the bus was threatening to turn over it would slide up against this wall and would help stop me. I leant forward to try to put some handbrake on to try and slow, but realised that the red light (which told me when the trolleys were on the wires) was out. To my relief the air brake worked. I stopped, got out, and saw that I had knocked the trolleys off another bus going up Bolton Road and smashed most of the street lights with mine! My regret was that I had not been able to see the spectacle as it occurred. I was proud of my thoughts in this emergency.

Another incident I remember was when working what was known as a Tea Time Special. This was overtime after working an early shift from 5 a.m. to 1 p.m. We worked overtime from about 4.15 to 6.30 p.m. to cover the evening rush. If your own conductor didn't want to work you teamed up with another driver and took it in turns to drive and conduct. A mate and I took a spare bus up to Greengates. Resting at the terminus we were nattering to each other with all the old dears earwigging, so we decided to lead them on.

'Are these buses easy to drive, Frank?' my mate asked.

'Dead easy.' I said. 'Just press the pedal to go and the other to stop.'

'Can I have a go?'

'No bother at all.' I said. 'Give me your cash bag and machine.' Having done that, my mate got in the cab and I rang the bell. He opened the emergency window and shouted 'Which way do we go, Frank?' You should have seen the rush of old dears getting off the bus!

One day I was working the 5.12am out of Bolton Depot to Eccleshill. We had to get to the depot fifteen minutes before starting and ring the Inspector at the Box in Forster Square. But my conductor had not turned up. So I rang the Inspector and booked my conductor in, took the bus out, stopped at the bottom of his road, ran up to his flat and knocked him up. I drove on to Eccleshill and picked him up on the way back down.

I was conducting one night going from Windhill to Thackley when the bus suddenly starting swerving all over the road. I went to the emergency window to find out what was wrong and the driver said 'I'm chasing a rabbit.' There, in the light of our headlights, was the poor little thing running like mad.

In the village of Saltaire was Dove Street where we sometimes reversed into to turn round. After turning we stood with about eight minutes standing time. There was a washing line across the street full of clean clothes. A dustbin waggon came along blowing his horn, to no avail. So he just drove through rubbing all the clothes on the top of the waggon. A lady came out, took all the washing in, and in the five minutes we stood there, washed all the clothes and hung them out to dry again.

My brother was courting a girl who lived near Eccleshill and one foggy night I was crawling my way up to Eccleshill when I saw him walking. I stopped to pick him up and he asked if he could have a go driving. I let him, and when we stopped by the Mechanics' he asked if he could turn it round. He set off too fast and I shouted to him to stop. He pressed what he thought was the clutch, but being a trolleybus it was the

Figure 8. Commercial Street, Shipley. *Dorothy Burrows*

power, and we nearly demolished Black Dan's, a fish shop on the corner.

After about two years I applied to drive motor buses and was allowed to start in the bus school. No more wires to worry about but buses also had their problems. We learnt on an old Guy bus which had a crash box and gear change which was the opposite way round to most cars; to select first gear you moved over to the right and up. There were two tests; one was taken after a number of lessons and you were allowed to put a couple of notches of handbrake on when changing down into first gear. You then did the permitting as we did on the trolleybuses, and then another test on a bus in service. Whilst permitting, the regular drivers had to go and sit upstairs and hope you did everything right and went on the right route. The buses we drove were mainly AECs with a pre-selector air change, and Daimlers, with a rather different pre-selector gear change, what I would call mechanical. The Daimler Utility buses had wooden seats and were very difficult to stop; the brake pedal was so stiff that you had to stand on it and change down into first to stop. One of my first bus driving experiences was driving on the Undercliffe route using AECs with a normal gear level but a pre-select box. The engines on these buses frequently boiled over. We used to have a water tap and watering can at Forster Square and I filled many a hot engine with cold water whilst on a tea time special. I often wonder what damage we did.

Driving the AECs was luxury compared to the Guys. They had air change gears and air brakes, but I was always terrified of what would happen if you had an air-line break; how would you stop! But they were a nice easy gear change were the AECs. The Daimlers were all right but had a stiffer clutch. If you didn't press the pedal right down it came back right up and would give your ankle a right crack! For some reason they used to put these old Daimlers on the Sandy Lane-Apperley Bridge route. We drivers feared this route; there was no time to change the gears and it was hard to stop the bus. We got to the bottom standing on the brakes!

In 1949 we got the Leylands. They were used on the Manchester Road. The first ones had a normal gear change but were quite a struggle and several ended up with broken gear sticks. Because everyone was then using pre-selectors, it was hard to change. Then the Crossleys came. They were used on the West Bowling route after the utility Daimlers. Some of the AECs had their pre-selectors with a gear lever change rather than a gear column change.

While acting as a spare driver we sometimes had to switch between trolleys and buses. It was hard to do both. Switching between two pedals and three and worrying about wires was hard, I can tell you. I remember seeing a bus stopped up Cheapside. I asked the driver what was wrong and he said he had forgotten how to drive it!

Once working on the Wrose to Fagley run with a Leyland, I was returning to the depot from Wrose and giving the bus full power down Kings Road knowing that if I drove fast I could run from Ludlam Street to catch the last bus to my home in Eccleshill and avoid the staff bus. At the terminus a passenger came down stairs and got off calling me a few rude names as he had banged his head on the roof as we were speeding down into town.

The time came when they wanted to close the smaller depots. My depot at Bolton was one of these. With only eighteen buses stationed there there was no work at times for the cleaners and fitters. The Bolton depot was built for trams and the doors were too narrow for

Figure 9. Karrier 'W' 713 reversing out of the Bolton depot on the day of its closure, 2 November 1958. *J.S. King*

the new eight foot wide vehicles, plus the fact that the buses had to reverse into a main road. The idea was to concentrate the buses at Thornbury. I was a union 'rep' at the time and organised protests agaianst the closures. But with working shifts it was difficult to organise meetings and there were few activists. We went to the Labour Group of the Council and were invited to a meeting of the Transport Commitee at the Town Hall. A compromise was reached whereby the deport was closed during the day and open in the early morning and evening. But it was closed eventually. (Figure 9) For the staff this was very hard, particularly working on early and late shifts, as it meant extra hours time travelling to and from work. It was with sadness I left the Transport Department in 1953.

An edited version by Bob Duckett of a taped recording of a talk given by Frank Long to a meeting of the Bradford Transport Association at the Pennington Midland Hotel , Bradford, on 8th May 1998.

8. The Flying Boats of Bradford

by Erik Blakeley, Kevin Cairns and Eugene Nicholson

IN 1972, A QUANTITY OF BLUEPRINTS was discovered concealed by a partition wall in the works of Christopher Pratt & Sons, a long-established firm of cabinet makers in Bradford. Christopher Pratt & Sons were engaged by the electrical engineers Phoenix Dynamo Manufacturing Company of Thornbury to make components for aeroplanes when Bradford Phoenix entered into a consortium led by Shorts and the Aircraft Manufacturing Company. The latter had links with De Havilland Aircraft Company Ltd. This article discusses the technological and social history of the early development of military aircraft design and the people of Bradford who had a part in it.

It is amazing that by 1919, only fifteen years after the Wright Brothers first flew a powered aeroplane, one of the largest aeroplanes could carry a load of 1,040 lbs 1000 miles at up to 94 mph flying 10,000 feet above sea-level.[1] The aeroplane, in question, was the Bradford-designed and built Phoenix Cork P5 flying boat (Figure 1).

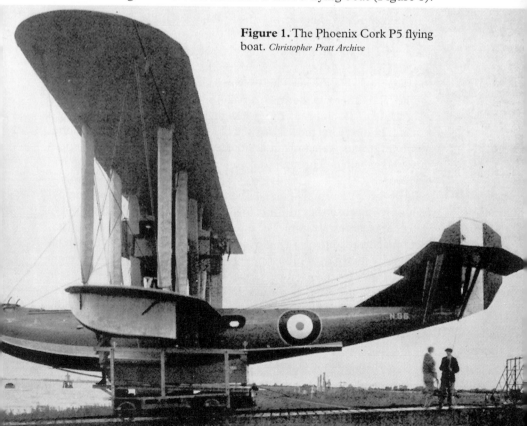

Figure 1. The Phoenix Cork P5 flying boat. *Christopher Pratt Archive*

It is sad that, as so often happens, it was the catalyst of war that accelerated the speed of technological development and that the intended load of the plane was, of course, bombs. Recognising such achievements are carried over into peace-time can reduce the sense of utter waste involved in the deaths of so many people. It is also tragic that the glut of aircraft at the end of the war meant that very few Corks ever flew and that the aircraft design and manufacturing skills developed in Bradford did not survive into civilian aeroplane manufacture.

In some ways, Bradford had come to symbolise the worst of the waste in lives and idealism of the First World War through the experiences of the 'Bradford Pals' battalions during the Battle of the Somme. It is, therefore, laudable to discuss the more positive achievements of the town in its support of the war effort and industry rather than just with the loss of life. It is strange that Bradford, one of the most landlocked towns in Britain, should become an important site for seaplane manufacture, but it is no odder than the fact that the town became a celebrated manufacturer of large castings for marine engine cylinders at about the turn of the century through the effort of Messrs. Thornton and Crebbin. These cylinders were up to 108 inches in diameter and 25 tons in weight and found their way into famous ships such as the battleship HMS *Thunderer* and battlecruiser HMS *Invincible*.[2]

There were two main problems in the way of developing effective aircraft. The first was the need to develop the understanding of the science of flight and the machinery that could generate the power needed. The second was the need for the appropriate skills to make the machines. Neither was an easy matter.

The vital difference between a balloon and an aeroplane is that the weight of a balloon or airship is less than that of the air occupying a similar volume. This means that the balloon floats. An aeroplane does not float. It must generate additional lift to get off the ground. It does this with its wings. Through trial and error the shape of the wing was developed.

Early internal combustion engines were lighter than steam engines primarily because they did not need a boiler and large amounts of water. The earliest examples of internal combustion engine cylinders were machined out of a single large block of metal. Steam engines and early internal combustion engines had low power-to-weight ratios. High power to weight ratios were crucial for aero-engines. In order to get airborne the engine had to accelerate the aeroplane to such a speed that the lift, supplied by the wings, equalled the weight of the aeroplane. The heavier the aeroplane the greater the take-off speed for a given wing design and angle to the airflow. At the time of the pioneers, the engine and the pilot would have been the heaviest components of the aeroplane, so a light engine was vital. Mercedes had developed a special lightweight engine for racing cars that used a separate steel forging for each cylinder welded together and surrounded by a pressed steel water jacket. Using this weight-saving idea and improving on it by, amongst other things, using aluminium pistons, Rolls Royce went on to design aero-engines including the Eagle, used on the Cork P5, and Hawk, used on the 'Longhorns' (see later) (Figure 2). They started design work in 1914.[3]

Figure 2. The Eagle engine in place on a Phoenix Cork P5. *Christopher Pratt Archive*

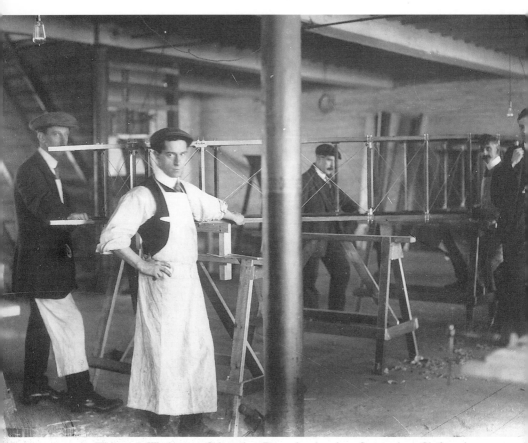

Figure 3. Workers at Cristopher Pratts by the aircraft strutting. Christopher Pratt, junior, who was in charge of the aircraft department, is on the right.
Christopher Pratt Archive

Bradford had influence during this period, not always recognised, in the development of Rolls Royce. A. H. Briggs, a Bradford man, bought a Rolls Royce car and was so impressed that he became a director. Possibly as a result of this Bradford came close to being the home of Rolls Royce in 1907 when the firm was considering moving from its, then, base in Manchester. The three candidates initially short-listed were Bradford, Coventry and Leicester, with an option to stay in Manchester. Leicester became the front runner, but out of nowhere Derby stole a march on them all through some very energetic salesmanship, and succeeded.[4]

Another man from the Bradford area who is seldom remembered is Mr A Smith who worked with Sopwith on the design of the famous

Sopwith Camel. He then, unfortunately, went on to work with the Japanese, then our allies, and saw his work used against the British and the Americans during World War Two.[5]

One of the best ways to produce a strong lightweight structure is to use a framework of triangulated struts supporting compressive loads and wires to support tensional loads with the whole structure covered with a lightweight covering (Figure 3). This required many carefully made joints and a lightweight raw material. Steel and aluminium tubing were becoming increasingly available and were being used more and more though wood was still a very good candidate. There were few established aeroplane makers but the skills of woodwork and upholstery which were required had been practised for generations by furniture makers such as Christopher Pratt & Sons. The framework was covered with linen fabric made rigid by doping. (Figure 4) The craftsmen joiners and specialist pioneering engineers were all working in fairly small groups. In order to generate the large numbers of aircraft needed to fight the First World War, collaboration would be required. It was also necessary to recruit and train new workers rapidly to meet the demand and

Figure 4. Ladies working on a wing section at the Christopher Pratt works. *Christopher Pratt Archive*

Figure 5. View of the Phoenix Dynamo Aircraft metal fitting shop,
Thornbury. *Christopher Pratt Archive*

replace men lost to the armed services. From a pre-war figure of
about three hundred the work force at Phoenix Dynamo reached a
peak of 4,500 in 1917 of which about 1,500 were women.[6] The
Phoenix Dynamo Manufacturing Company were credited with
particular success in recruiting and training due to a system
developed by P.J.Pybus, the Managing Director. His success in
introducing inexperienced labour in engineering factory work,
especially women, led to his being asked by Lloyd George to
undertake a lecture tour and to write an account of the employment
of female workers in engineering workshops. This was circulated, as
a guide, for other employers. It is clear that women workers were
considered something of an alien commodity and invariably
segregated (Figure 5). Bearing this point in mind it is not surprising
that Phoenix Dynamo Manufacturing Company built a special
canteen . Twenty thousand copies of *Women on Munitions of War* were
printed by the Ministry of Munitions in 1918. For one of the female
workers that answered the call of her country, this led to the founding
of a family tradition.

Mrs Edith Smith who worked in the aircraft Fitting Department of
Phoenix Dynamo Manufacturing Company had a son, Mr F.L.
Smith, who went on to work for English Electric for forty years and

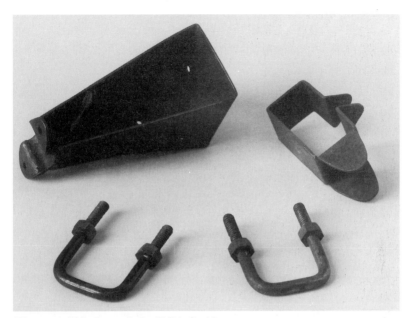

Figure 6. U bolts made by Edith Smith. *Mr F.L. Smith*

retired as Traction Production Officer in 1972. He still has some of the aircraft components his mother made such as steel flanges for joining wooden components, U bolts and the triangular brass badges marked 'On War Service' which were used as a security passes to the works (Figures 6 and 7). For his mother to have kept these demonstrates both the importance she placed on her work on the

Figure 7. Brass badges worn for identification by workers at the Bradford Phoenix works bearing the inscription 'On War Service'. *Mr F.L. Smith*

Figure 8. Mrs Edith Smith (standing) with her mother and brothers. *Mr F.L.Smith*

aeroplanes and her pride in the skills she learnt.[7] (Figure 8)

A contemporary woman's perspective on the issue can be gained by reading the article by O.E. Monkhouse presented as a paper to the Institution of Mechanical Engineers.[8] In her introduction she implies a link between the employment of women in munition factories and the granting of the franchise to women. She also indicates that there were problems within the male workforce accepting the presence of

Figure 9. Female engineering worker measuring a part. *Christopher Pratt Archive*

female workers and in adapting management styles to suit women.

According to her, there were about a million women employed in the munition factories in 1918 which included the aircraft industry (she used an unnamed aircraft works as an example in making one of her points). Her final paragraph is especially interesting when considered alongside the present debate concerning single and working mothers. She concludes by saying:

> It must be remembered that a woman's work is not ended when she leaves the factory. On her largely depends the life and happiness of the nation in creating and developing a happy healthy family life and it is her privilege to care for the physical and spiritual welfare of the race. Added industrial efficiency therefore at the expense of women fulfilling their primary duties in their homes and to their children cannot result in anything but national disaster, and it is a sacred duty of the State to ensure that women are only used as wealth producers in so far as it does not affect the healthy development of the race.

The manufacture of complex machinery to uniform designs by numerous companies made vital the use of accepted standards of length and their fine measurement. V.I. Norbury Williams discussed this and its effects on the War effort in a paper published by the Bradford Engineering Society in 1921.[9] In this he describes how a mainly female workforce was involved in the skilled measurement of screw threads (Figure 9).

The Phoenix Dynamo Manufacturing Company grew from a series of take-overs and amalgamations starting in 1895 with a take-over of the Wray Electrical Engineering Company of the Soho Works, Thornton Road, Bradford. Some expansion of the company followed and then a competitor in the field of electrical engineering, Rosling and Fynn, closed in 1903 enabling Phoenix Dynamo to buy the works in Thornbury, Bradford. Phoenix Dynamo were by now specialising in the manufacture of heavy electrical machinery for the mining and textile industries. They were, therefore, well placed for the manufacture of armaments when war came. A contact with the Cammell Laird shipbuilding firm led to contracts for artillery shells of which they made over a million before the war ended. This established their credentials with the Ministry of Supply and so they were invited to join a four-company consortium to build aeroplanes. An Aircraft Department was set up within Phoenix Dynamo under Captain J. C. Crawshaw with Mr E. Stronach as manager. Mr Stronach had worked for the British and Colonial Aeroplane Company of Bristol.

The first important project that came to Bradford was the *Short 184* seaplane, also known as the *Short 225* because of its 225 horse-power Sunbeam engine. This was in 1915.

Twelve of these were ordered from the Phoenix Dynamo Manufacturing Company. In order to get the appropriate knowledge as quickly as possible, a group of draughtsman, from the various companies making the *Short 184*, were sent to Rochester and Eastchurch on the Isle of Grain. This included Leonard Brown from Phoenix Dynamo.[10] They proceeded to measure an existing *Short 184* and studied its design at length. Each produced drawings of certain parts of the aeroplane that were consequently copied for the others so that all the firms had sets of complete drawings.

The fact that the planes of World War One were trying to carry heavy weaponry, especially bombs and torpedoes, meant that they were constantly pushing their technology to the very limits. *Short 184s* from the seaplane carrier HMS *Ben-my-Chree* in the Eastern Mediterranean, had several problems. Firstly the aeroplanes found they could only get airborne during the cool of the morning. The hot air at noon would be less dense causing two problems. The first is that the lift provided by the less dense air and the thrust produced by the propeller would be less and second, the smaller amount of air taken into each engine cylinder, would marginally reduce the horsepower of the engine.

Modern car engines reduce this problem using intercoolers, turbochargers and superchargers. The next problem was that their effective ceiling was so low that they could not get over the low hills of Judah. Finally, the engines had to run at very high temperatures; so high that, although they ran well as long as they were kept going continuously, the valves got so hot that they warped on cooling. This required the engine to be stripped and given new valves after each flight. The aircraft were kept in the air by replacing the complete engine with a spare after each flight whilst the valves were changed ready for the engine to go into another aeroplane. The air crew had to face all this before even attempting to fight the enemy.[11]

Phoenix Dynamo reissued its drawings to Christopher Pratt and Sons of Bradford. Christopher Pratts can be traced back to 1845 after the first Christopher Pratt had completed his apprenticeship with the cabinet maker and philanthropist Joseph Nutter.

The larger aeroplanes built in Bradford, including the flying boats, were assembled in the Belle Vue Barracks drill hall off Manningham Lane. Other specialist wood-working firms were also involved including Ramsey's of Dockfield, a barge builder and

Figure 10. A Short 184 torpedo bomber. The 'Phoenix, Bradford' mark can be seen above the tail float. *Christopher Pratt Archive*

Webster's of Leeds Road, Windhill, another furniture maker.[12] There is speculation that work was also undertaken by Enoch Shaw and Sons on North Parade as well as Uriah Woodheads.[13] (Figure 10)

The chief designer at Phoenix Dynamo was W. O. Manning who had a service background and had been involved in aviation experiments as early as 1908. Even so this only gave him six years experience before war broke out. The two senior draughtsmen of most interest in this account have, unfortunately, the same initials which make attribution of initialled drawings somewhat difficult, but not impossible as the handwritings are different. The two, in question, are Mr Leonard Brown and Mr L Barradell. Brown who was the chief draughtsman for Phoenix Dynamo had little or no experience of aircraft design before his trip to Shorts to participate in the drawing of the *Short 184*. He remained with the company throughout the war and retired in 1954 from what had by then become English Electric (Figure 11).

The career of Barradell was more mobile as he was at Brush Electrical Engineering Company in Loughborough at the start of the war work, however the presence of his initials and signature on some of the drawings, originating from the drawing office of Phoenix Dynamo Manufacturing Company, suggests that he spent part of the war in Bradford.

The first Bradford-built *Short 184* flew from Great Yarmouth on January 28th 1916. This was less than a year after Phoenix Dynamo had been asked to enter the aeroplane-making business. In all, a total of about six hundred and fifty *Short 184s* and their variants were built for the R.N.A.S of which only fifty eight were built by Phoenix Dynamo. Of the grand total of 938 *Short 184s* Phoenix built sixty two. Phoenix Dynamo Manufacturing Company of Bradford, Brush Electrical Engineering Company of Loughborough and Robey's of Lincoln undertook to make the Maurice Farman S7 ' Longhorn' under licence from the Aircraft Manufacturing Company who held the manufacturing rights from the French-born English designers. Brush would appear to have produced an English set of drawings from which the companies worked. The 'Longhorn' was a very small machine with little or no offensive capability. It was intended as a trainer. Although it was a land plane 'Longhorns' made by Phoenix Dynamo and Christopher Pratt & Sons were going to the Royal Navy.

The Maurice Farman S7 'Longhorn' was built in such numbers that it was regarded as the 'bread and butter' of the Phoenix Dynamo

Figure 11. Leonard Brown, Chief Draughtsman at Phoenix Dynamo Aircraft Division with a model of the Cork flying boat. *Yorkshire Evening Post 28 December 1964*

Manufacturing Company war effort. This was reflected in the fact that it was nicknamed the 'Mechanical Cow' as well as the 'Rumpety' by its workers.

At least thirty of these were powered by Rolls Royce Hawk engines.(14) This six-cylinder shared several characteristics with the larger V12 Eagle engine including cylinders of the same size and generating 75 hp.[15] From accounts of engine failures it would also seem that the Renault 90 hp engines were fitted to Phoenix-built 'Longhorns'.[16] The authors, however, share doubt as to whether this is correct.

Other aeroplanes were manufactured by Phoenix Dynamo and Christopher Pratts and drawings for some of them survive:

Maurice Farman S7 'Longhorn' trainer	190 drawings
Short 184 seaplane and its 225 Bomber derivative	253 drawings
Felixstowe F3 flying boat	89 drawings
Felixstowe F5 flying boat	63 drawings
Phoenix 'Cork' P5 flying boat	6 drawings
FK10 quadruplane fighter	201 drawings

Phoenix Dynamo did try to produce a commercial flying boat called the *'Pulex'* but did not make a success of civilian aeroplane manufacture in the hard times straight after the war. For a time, between the wars, flying boats were seen as the best means of

Figure 12. Moving the dis-assembled aircraft wings from the Christopher Pratt's works to the Phoenix Dynamo works at Thornbury. They would later be moved, by horse, to the coast, and re-assembled again. *Christopher Pratt Archive*

producing large passenger aircraft. Firstly a large flying boat could afford to take a very large take-off run whereas land planes are restricted by runway lengths.

Secondly, for trips across seas and oceans, flying boats had the advantage that they could land anywhere en route in the event of mechanical problems.

The history of aircraft manufacture in Bradford is one which deserves remembering as it demonstrates the skill and adaptability of the industries and workforce of the city. (Figure 12)

Acknowledgements:

The authors would like to thank the Bradford Industrial Museum for access to the collection of Blueprints, the Christopher Pratt Archive, Barry and David Pratt for the loan of numerous publications and unpublished material, Mr F. L. Smith for the loan of articles associated with his family history, and Ian Ward for photography.

References

1. Dixon, C., 'Flying Boats made in Bradford', *Dalesman,* Dalesman Publishing Co., Vol. 22, pp 245-246, 1961
2. Banks, J.W., 'The Progress of Engineering in Bradford' *Journal of Proceedings of Bradford Engineering Society,* Twenty-seventh session 1925-26, 1926
3. Gunston, W., 'The Classic Aero, Engine', *Aeroplane Monthly,* IPC Business Press Ltd, October, pp 562-565, 1982
4. Evans, M., Personal Communication, Head of Corporate Heritage, Rolls Royce PLC, 1982
5. Walsh, J., Personal Communication, 1998
6. Banks *see above*
7. Smith, F.L., Personal Communication, 1998 (son of E.A. Smith, a worker in the Aircraft Fitting Deptment of Bradford Phoenix, and President of English Electric Veterans Association.)
8. Monkhouse, O.E., 'The Employment of Women in Munition Factories', *The Journal of the Institution of Mechanical Engineers,* No. 4 April, 1918
9. Norbury Williams, Y.I., 'Fine Measurement in Engineering Workshops' *Journal of Proceedings of Bradford Engineering Society,* Twenty-second session 1920-1921, 1921
10. Rowley, A., 'The Plane Makers of Bradford', *Yorkshire Evening Post,* 28th December, 1964
11. Grey, C.G., *Sea Flyers,* Faber and Faber, 1942
12. Francis, W.G., Personal Communication (friend of the youngest of Ramsey's children, born 1911), 1998
13. Green, F., Personal Communication (relative of employee of Enoch Shaw & Sons), 1998
14. Robertson, B., *British Military Aircraft Serials 1911-1971,* Ian Allen, 1971, p152
15. Gunston *ibid*
16. Dixon *ibid*

9. BRADFORD'S ITALIANS

by Fredrick Taglione

SINCE 1914, ONE HUNDRED MILLION PEOPLE have been killed as a direct result of war. In the years since then many millions of the family members of those killed have been left with traumas not easily forgotten.

Yet these senseless tragic killings were not the end of the suffering. For instance in 1946, after the Second World War, there were twelve million refugees in Europe alone. These were the men, women and children, including the elderly and infirm, who had been torn from their homes, fleeing for their very lives, to face a despairing journey to nowhere. They lost everything they had worked and saved for. The future they had planned was gone forever.

They became an unwanted race of people. No country wanted them or could afford them. As they searched for somewhere to live, successive government 'propaganda specialists' accused them of thieving, and called them scavengers. It was a perfect excuse to refuse them entry into their country.

This couldn't go on indefinitely and finally, throughout Europe, refugee camps were set up and the refugees were segregated according to their nationality to prevent fighting. The name given to these camps were 'displaced persons camps' and the refugees became known as DPs. This title robbed them of what little dignity they had left.

Most of the refugees were skilled tradesmen: joiners, plumbers, electricians, builders, toy-makers and shoe repairers. The womenfolk were dressmakers, midwives, cooks and chefs. There were farmers' wives, used to early hours and hard work. Now here they all were, laid idle in these massive DP camps.

Eventually Western countries began to realise they needed workers to replace those killed in the wars, so the camps began to empty. Tens of thousands came to England, others went to America, Canada, Australia, and South Africa. Many stayed in Germany, France and Holland, all settling down to new lives.

What happened to these people? What problems did they face, what work did they do, what kind of entertainment did they enjoy?

I am the offspring of a refugee family which was part of that Italian community that flooded into England in the late nineteenth century. Prior to the Italians were the Germans and the Irish who arrived in Bradford between 1817 to 1850, settling around the Bolton and Wapping Road area, now known as Little Germany.

In 1865 a young man called Joseph Cadamateri came to Bradford and stayed. He was eighteen years of age and must have been one of the first Italian immigrants. As his sons grew up they returned to Italy on holiday or business, and they would tell the young Italians of how Bradford was the textile capital of the world, a worker's paradise undergoing an Industrial Revolution with work for all. His message spread by word of mouth and from 1876 to 1920 Italians came and settled in Bradford in their thousands. The majority of Italians arrived in Bradford in the 1880s coming from all areas of Italy, from Milan, Turin, Rome, Naples and Florence. Many thousands came from dried-up villages and impoverished urban areas.

Why do I describe them as 'dried-up' villages? Refugees were not the only casualties of the aftermath of war. Starting in 1797 with the rise of Napoleon Bonaparte, till his death in 1820, Europe was deluged with blood, killing and drought. For the following sixty years Europe never settled down. There were wars in Hungary, Austria, Russia, Prussia, Italy and so on. What was the cost of these wars in Europe? Winston Churchill, referring to World War Two, told us that it cost one million pounds a

Figure 1. Andrea Verischer was born in Italy. Wearing clogs, cord trousers and a grey jacket, this young man was a street musician living in Albert Street in Otley Road when painted by John Sowden in 1888. *Bradford Art Galleries, Museums and Libraries*

day to keep the war alive. So one can imagine the cost of eighty years of war in Europe.

War is just as costly in human terms. As one war ended and surviving soldiers, wounded or otherwise, returned home to their parents' farms where they found poverty, worthless land, no money to buy seeds, their parents (only in their forties) starving to death, only to find another war starting up somewhere else. It wasn't long before many young men and women got a train to Calais, a boat to England, then on to Canada or America. Some came back to Italy and, like Joseph Cadamateri, they would tell their relatives and friends about work, food and money. You can imagine the reaction, there began a mass migration of Europeans going west.

We've watched many films and read many accounts of the wagon trains from the 1820s onwards trekking Europeans towards

Figure 2. Mary Schager was of Italian origin and told her fortunes in the fairs and market places of Victorian Bradford. Dressed in a blue skirt and apron, white blouse with full sleeves, and her head covered by a red and black scarf, she posed for John Sowden in May 1888. *Bradford Art Galleries, Museums and Libraries*

California. These were the youth of Europe: they weren't going to lie down and die. They had that pioneer spirit: however hard the sea journey, however hard the trek across Indian country, they had the determination to find a new life. And now once again the youth of Europe made their way to England. Many made it, many didn't, but these pioneers opened the gates of Europe to have an opportunity to live, to work, to plan a future for their families. A goal worth fighting for.

But how could they make these journeys when they were so poor? The answer is that the whole family would contribute the fare for one son or daughter, and when that one got to America or England and found work, they in turn would send money home. In many cases it worked, but not in all. Some young women got pregnant and had to return home. Some young men were provoked into fights and ended up in prison.

Because of these problems it became advantageous to travel and live with a group of your own race, and hence the ghettos. Whether it is Jewish, Irish, Italian, Russian or German, if a lot of the same nationality live as one group, it is called a ghetto.

As you can imagine, not everyone could face the sea crossing from Liverpool to New York, so these stayed in England. Some stayed in the sea ports of France, Belgium and Holland.

The first Taglione to come to Bradford was my grandfather's sister, Maria Juliet, and for us that is when it all started.

Who Were We?

Between 1876 and 1920 Italians came and settled in Bradford in their thousands. I was born into the third generation of the Taglione family and as a young boy I was always curious as to why our customs were different from the other children at school, so I used to badger my poor old dad with questions. It was my Father who told me about Joseph Cadamateri.

My Mother always used to believe that to rest is to rot or rust and Joseph Caddy, as he was later known, must have felt the same way. He hired a handcart, made some ice cream and put it in a tub stacked with ice. He would put this on the cart and went around the streets of Bradford selling his ice creams. 'Did he make a living doing that?' I asked. My Dad replied 'Well he had fourteen children and set them all up in his business creating an empire.' In fact 'Caddy's' ices are still going strong in Dewsbury after 133 years! I asked my Dad how he know all this and he answered 'Because my cousin Ernest Cervi married one of the grand-daughters.' The Beniditos, the

Bachicaupo brothers and the Chiconis all rented 'Caddy' carts and sold ice cream on commission.

My Dad went on to relate some of the family heads that lived in Bradford. He mentioned the Ventos, the Diffouris, the Mollicones, the Cervis or Chervis, the Tenzios, the Sinicolas, the Verrechis, the Cappuvanis, the Neros, the Steffanutis, the Donnatellis, the Minchellas, the Falkerellis, the Tagliones, the Maratz, the Duce and the Romanis. He said there were many more. All these names were single families, mostly brothers or brothers and sisters. Forty years later when I was about six years old these names had quadrupled; I remember five families of Diffouris, three families of Mollicones and in my particular family there were three families of Tagliones. And this despite the hundreds of Italian girls who lost their family names through marriage. Most Italian girls married Irish lads.

My grandfather's sister, Maria Juliet Taglione left her home village of Arpino, a small mountain village south of Rome and north of Naples. She was about sixteen when she left. Whether she came over with a Mr Cervi or alone we are not sure, but she eventually married Giovanni Cervi. (Figure 3) Her husband Giovanni was a top-class musician. He used to make, repair and teach the piano accordion. We have a picture of Aunt Juliet sitting on a wall outside Peel Park up Otley Road playing a piano accordion one summer evening. She must have been about 22 years old in the picture.

Aunt Juliet was born in 1868 and lived into the 1960s. She must have arrived in Bradford in 1884. Her brother Angelo, my grandfather, followed her to England leaving Arpino behind. He first settled in Manchester, then on a visit to friends in Leeds he met a Miss Rosalie Donnatelli who was from a village called Zora about six miles from Arpino. A relationship developed so

Figure 3. Maria Taglione painted by John Sowden in 1890. *Bradford Art Galleries, Mueums and Libraries*

Figure 4. My father and his parents, Angelo and Rosalie, 1912. *F Taglione*

he got work in Bradford and lived in Paper Hall Street with his sister
Juliet.

Both Angelo and Rosalie were born in 1865 and were 25 years old
when they married at St Mary's Church in East Parade. (Figure 4)
Many Italians worked in the iron foundries of Bradford making
castings for the textile machinery, but Grandad Angelo didn't care

Figure 5. Italian 'tingelary' man with performing monkeys. Peckover Street c.1890. *Bradford Heritage Recording Unit*

for this kind of work. So he would walk down to North Wing and hire a barrel organ from Carlo and Madeleine. He would then push it down Church Bank and across over to Peckover Street in Little Germany. There he would play up to 40 or 50 tunes of that era, sometimes for as long as eight to ten hours. Then he would return the barrel organ, or Tingelary as it was better known, pay his rent and return the two monkeys he had hired, and that was one day's work. (Figure 5) Another day he would go with old Mr Mollicone and sell ice cream. He did this seven days a week until his wedding in 1890.

Angelo and Rosie had ten children, six girls and four boys up to 1904. All the girls died, some were stillborn, some died of diphtheria. Anthony, the oldest boy was born about 1892, Nicholas in 1897, then my Father Cisino, or Chisino, in 1899, and the youngest was born in 1901. These sons survived. As a matter of interest all four sons served in the British Army in the First World War and were in the Battle of the Somme. (Figure 6) Yet after the war they were still called 'bloody foreigners' by bigots. Luckily all four sons survived the war and came home to marry and have families.

My Uncle Anthony married an Italian woman called Alexandrina Sinicola around 1916; they had two children, Mary and Peter. Uncle Nicholas married an English woman called Rosie Hodgson around

Figure 6. My Dad, 1916. *F.Taglione*

1920. (Figure 7) Rosie came from the Manchester Road area. They had seven children.

After Anthony and Nicholas married, my Father Chisino was left at home to work and care for his elderly parents and his brother John, who came out of the army disabled. He was under a great deal of pressure; he was 24 years old and wanted to get married and have his own family. After the war there were many lonely girls and young widows. He was a good catch and he had many tempting offers, but his Mother chased them away. She would say 'All the Italian and Irish girls want you to get them pregnant and then you will have to marry them.' My Father knew this wasn't true, but he would get depressed listening to them moan. However, unknown to his parents, he had a friend called Tommy Zaccadelli who used to go to Glasgow once a fortnight to buy pasta in bulk from an Italian warehouse, and on one of these visits he met a young unmarried Italian girl called Amelia. She was 23 years old and very intelligent, doing business studies in the evenings. When Tommy suggested to my Father that he should go with him one weekend, my Father readily agreed. He was introduced to Amelia and then for six months they exchanged letters, but it was done through his friend Tommy because my Father knew his Mother would have torn the letters up. A year later my Father and Amelia were married. (Figure 8) Although his brothers Anthony and Nicholas supported him, his mother, Rosalie,

Figure 7. Uncle Nicholas and Rosie, 1920. *F.Taglione*

hated Amelia for no reason, even threatening to kill her at the first opportunity, and she never spoke to my mother for seven years, right up to my grandmother's death in 1930.

Figure 8. My parents in 1923. F.Taglione

Chisino or Charlie as he was now being called, and Amelia, had a happy marriage, and one year later they had a son who they called Angelo. Being a first grandson my grandmother spoiled him dreadfully, and because she hated my mother so much, if she attempted to chastise Angelo in any way, grandmother would scream 'If you lay finger on young Angelo I'll cut your throat'.' But just before Grandma died in 1930 she begged my mother to forgive her, which she naturally did.

When Angelo was four years old and my mother was almost three months pregnant with me she had to return to Italy to sort out some land taxes etc. She went in April 1928 for six months, taking Angelo with her, and of course all her relations there made a fuss of him so that he became quite spoiled. However once all the legalities to her land and property had been sorted out she returned home. My Dad, who had not wanted her to go to Italy in that condition, had missed her terribly. He was worried sick and couldn't wait to get her to hospital as she was almost full term with me. Two weeks after she arrived home I was born. My Dad told me later that she had said 'You took Angelo off me but this one's mine. His name is Frederick, after my father, and you can forget your Mother's ideas.' So that is how I appeared on the scene. (Figure 9)

Figure 9. The author aged 16, in the army, April 1945. *F. Taglione*

A year later my sister Margaret was born, a gorgeous black-haired brown-eyed beauty. Sadly after Margaret was born my Mother spent almost all of the next eight years in and out of hospital with long stays because of high blood pressure which was a killer in those days. She died in 1938 leaving a husband and three children.

So far I have related to you the history of the Taglione family from 1884 when Aunt Juliet arrived in Bradford. But of course many of the daughters changed their name on marriage and many of the sons married English girls, and in the process many lost their identity and forgot their Italian roots.

If we compare the third generation Taglione's from Uncle Anthony and Auntie Sandrini we can see how this happened; their daughter Mary Taglione became on marriage Mary Mulqueen, their son Peter married a Margaret Dracup. From Uncle Nicholas and Auntie Rosie, their eldest daughter Rosie became Rosie Waddington, their daughter Mary became Mary Broadbent, Florence became Florence Brooks, Annie became Annie Gledhill, Nicholas Junior married Ada Norton, Fred married Dorren Smith and Bernard married Margaret Poulter. From my father and mother Chisino and Amelia, Angelo, the eldest, married Betty Butcher, Frederick, that's me, married Elly Kleiss and my sister Margaret married Norman Toney.

If it has been possible to relate this history of my family one wonders about the other Italian families I have mentioned. They all have their own stories to tell about the changes that were made throughout the three generations: We went to school together, played together, grew up together. I sometimes wonder how many stopped being Italian, how many changed their names, and how many young ones now who are not even aware that they are descendants of Italian refugees!

By 1934 I was six years old, and even at that young age I could see the many changes that were taking place. Girls of fourteen were working full time in the textile mills; you didn't see many women wearing long black dresses that reached the floor. Teenage girls wore brightly coloured knee length skirts and dresses; they wore silk stockings and had ribbons in their hair. I remember cousins Rosie, Mary and Florrie trying to dance the 'Charleston', the latest craze.

If you were lucky enough to get a two bedroomed back-to-back house it cost three shillings a week rent and gas lighting on a gas meter. If you didn't smoke or drink you could survive comfortably.

The area we lived in was quite close to the Catholic Church, St Mary's in East Parade. But with Bradford being a mainly Quaker-run city the Catholic Church had to struggle to survive. In the 1850s a Catholic Bishop struggled for years for survival, exhausting all his own funds, and in the end he had to leave the city a failure. But the Irish and Italian immigrants of the 1870s to 1890s breathed new life into the Catholic Church.

At St Mary's there was also a Church Hall and a school built in East Parade, and this is where the immigrant children went to school. On Sunday there were four masses, and on Saturday evening a relaxing whist drive and dance. This new religious way of life caught on and it helped to keep the peace. The only problem was all the Italians were Roman Catholic whereas the Irish were Irish Catholics, and no one dare say otherwise! It was a sore point, but as all eight priests were Irish, we gave in.

Girls were taught in a separate school in Jermyn Street off Stott Hill next to the Infant's school. The girls school was run by Nun teachers. Some were loving and kind, some were strict, but all were firm. They had to be, they were dealing with girls from broken homes, drunken fathers, etc.

Little Italy

On the Cathedral side of Church bank, just above the Cathedral was Stott Hill. At one time there was a magnificent Manor House called Stott Hill House. The owner at one time was a military man called

Captain Priestley. As the mills were being erected on Bolton Road, Wapping Road and North Street, houses were being built for the workers; these were back-to-back dwellings. Two of the streets were called Captain Street and Priestley Street after Captain Priestley. As time went on Stott Hill House fell into disrepair and ended up a 'doss house' for immigrant Irish labourers until they found proper dwellings, and then it was shamefully demolished in the early 1900s.

Going up Otley Road on the left hand side were a series of street names that were named after the Stuarts; for example King Charles Street, King Charles Court, Cavalier Street, Cavalier Court. There were also a Wellington Street and a Nelson Street. This was the area in which the Italians lived and survived in the 1880s onwards. It became a densely populated area housing thousands of immigrant families, both Irish and Italian.

Around this time, apart from Joseph Cadamateri's influence in 1865, what other influence was there of Italian origin? Some of the buildings in Little Germany were Italian Gothic styles built by Italian architects; one in particular is the Law Russell House in Vicar Lane. Also in the 1830s to the 1860s, Italian architects came to Bradford buying tons of Bradford quarry stone, exporting it to Italy to build palaces and magnificent church buildings. Other Italian influences in Bradford was the well known jewellers, Fattorini's, and other business associates.

Bradford in the 1890s and early 1900s could offer immigrants not only work but education and a new way of life, but above all a future, and this is why many stayed, including my grandparents. Looking back at the area we lived in it could be called 'Little Italy'. After all we already had 'Little Germany' and later the Manchester Road area became known as 'The Irish Channel'. We were fast becoming a Cosmopolitan city.

I have already mentioned my grandfather going around the streets of Bradford with a barrel-organ, known at the time as a 'Tingelary'. Other Italians did the same, and eventually they became known as 'Organ-Grinders'. Nevertheless they would play 30 or 40 popular melodies of that time, *Rosie of Tralee, When Irish Eyes are Smiling, Just a Little Bit of Heaven,* to name but a few. As they played the children would dance and the mothers would sing along, and for half an hour it took the worry of poverty away. Grandad would then send his companion around with a cap for a few coins and then he would move on. One had to have a companion to help push the 'Tingalary' up the steep streets of Bradford. My father told me that in the summer, grandfather would sell ice-cream, but he added 'All his four sons hated bank Holiday Monday when their Dad sold ice-cream', because Angelo would start the day at 6 am making the ice-cream, at 8.30 the four sons would have to push two hand carts full of ice-cream packed in tubs of ice and placed on the handcarts with sacks to keep it cool. They would push the carts with grandad walking in front down King Charles Street, North Wing, North Street and Stott Hill into Bolton Road, then down on the Canal Road and all the way to Shipley and finally push the carts up to Shipley Glen, usually getting there by 9.45 am. They then put both tubs onto one cart and leave their Dad and young John, who was eight, to sell the ice-cream while the other three sons, Anthony, Nicholas and Chisino took the handcarts back to King Charles Street, get a refill and set off back to the Glen, doing this two or three times a day. Of course these three sons dare not refuse, but they used to pray incessantly for rain, but no such luck. Yet on a good day Grandad could make £1 for the effort which was the equivalent to two week's work. And when you think, a cornet full of ice-cream cost one half-penny, and a sandwich one penny, you had to sell a lot of ice-cream to make anything, but it worked.

My Dad told me that when he was a boy at school he remembered an old Italian called Isador who used to roam the streets of Bradford selling broken biscuits in bulk form at wholesale prices. He used to buy them from a Leeds Italian wholesaler called 'Vadonis'. Another time I remember my Dad telling me that the oldest Italians in Bradford were the 'Bachicaupos', nicknamed by the children as simply 'Bass'.

I also remember him telling me that from the *Cock & Bottle* public house to Peel Park both sides of the street were lined with shops selling all kinds of merchandise, and with a pretty girl by your side you could spend four hours looking in the shops, first up one side, then down the other. (Figure 10)

Note. *This account is part of an unpublished story of Frederick Taglione's life. A copy of the full story is in Bradford Libraries. Editor*

Figure 10. Little now remains of 'Little Italy'. The Cock & Bottle is swamped by tower blocks and the six-lane 'freeway'. *Bob Duckett*

10. KEIGHLEY PRIDE

by John Waddington-Feather

When I was young and the sap ran high
as wayward as the moon;
the town and valley throbbed with life
which glowed like the sun at noon;
then time stretched out a winding lane,
un-ending, out of sight;
where youth and time went on and on,
like stars on cloudless night.

But now that I'm old and dry as a stick,
and plod like my doggerel rhyme,
the town and the valley are changed, quite changed,
transformed with me by time;
for only crumbling shells remain,
dead as my manhood's rut;
and ghosts slink through the familiar ways
where I used to swagger and strut.

'A Tale from the West Riding' in *Wild Tales from the West,* by John Waddington-Feather

Editor's Introduction

Keighley fascinates me. I pass through it frequently. At first it was a matter of finding somewhere to park or cursing the long walk between rail and bus stations, particularly when trying to cross the busy Bradford Road or dodging the cars coming out of entrances to the many supermarkets and the multi-story car park. But familiarity brought a growing awareness of the magnificent architecture of the buildings, of fascinating glimpses through archways, snickets and backstreets, of a character all its own. I started to linger longer and made a point of always having a camera with me. And then I met playwright, teacher, clergyman, poet and raconteur, John Waddington-Feather. This genial 'dry stick' is Keighley born and bred, and despite living and working away from his home town, he regularly visits his beloved Keighley.

So with a camera in one pocket and a notebook in the other, I was led on an entertaining, educational and inspirational tour of a very surprising place. This is not a history of Keighley, nor is it Keighley in old photographs: it is one person's memories stimulated by what can be seen today. John is proud of Keighley. Just look around, and share his pride! We start at Cliffe Castle.

Figure 1. Detail from Cliffe Castle Museum

When I first knew Cliffe Castle it was a very run-down place. I remember just after the war, a group of us lads found a cache of wine in the derelict grounds. We got very drunk! Cliffe Castle later became a museum having been bought for the town in 1949 by Sir Bracewell Smith. (Figure 1). He once invited a train-load of Keighley schoolchildren to the Mansion House in London when he was its Lord Mayor.

I got to know this museum very well when it was moved from the old mansion in Victoria Park. They talk about deprived kids. We were deprived of many luxuries down Lawkholme Lane, but I never regarded myself as deprived of education or educational facilities. With such great paintings, furniture, exhibits, a magnificent Carnegie Library, how could we possibly be deprived? Working class we may have been, but this was all part of our culture and we took it for granted. I came to the museum often, away from the distractions of a crowded home, and into a wider world, a world whose horizons spanned continents.

It was our world too! And we added to it. My father, Ira Feather, an auctioneer, donated several items, including a stuffed white owl and an eighteenth century wine glass; while the paratrooper National Service uniform of Second Lieutenant John Waddington-Feather is here somewhere!

In my boyhood Keighley had a great cultural life. We had an orchestra, an art club, little theatre, operatic group, a literature and

Figure 2. Temple Street and the old Methodist Church

natural history society. We got to hear world-famous singers like Kathleen Ferrier, Gwen Catley, Owen Brannigan and Norman Walker. They appeared as soloists with massed Keighley choirs at Temple Street Methodist Church, the biggest church in Keighley, where oratorios like The Messiah were performed annually (Figure 2). In his autobiography, Denis Healey recalls that the Keighley Hippodrome had annual visits from the D'Oyly Carte Opera playing Gilbert and Sullivan, and from other dramatic companies:

> *I remember Sir Frank Benson hamming Shakespeare with his skinny shanks, the melodramatic declamations of Donald Wolfit and the poetic baritone of Ion Swinley. My real favourite, however, was Tod Slaughter as Sweeney Todd, the Demon Barber of Fleet Street.*

Keighley also had its Silver Prize Band and its own Salvation Army Band. It was a vibrant place with activities of all kinds, from dog racing to classical drama productions.

Between Cliffe Castle and the Skipton Road was an area where the rich lads used to live, some were from Belgium and other countries.

Figure 3. 'Upper Crustia', Skipton Road.

(Figure 3) Many of the families which lived here and nearby Utley were in the wool trade and had great wealth: the 'Upper Crustians' I called them.

At the start of the Skipton Road was the Boys' Grammar School. The Keighley Boys' Grammar School was part of a larger complex which housed a dance-hall (our lunchtime dining hall), a fine stage (where two productions a year were staged and prizes given from at Speech Day), a technical college, and a School of Art. The Grammar School in its heyday was one of the country's finest, sending boys each year to Oxbridge and all the other universities in England, of which there were only nine when I was at school. It produced such scholars as Dr Gordon Bottomley, Sir Herbert Butterfield and Lord Asa Briggs, not to mention scores of professors and university lecturers throughout the world.

Figure 4. 'Middle Crustia'. The street where Lord Healey lived as a boy.

Between the Skipton Road and the railway is an area I call Middle Crustia. Officially it is named Showfield, after the field where agricultural shows used to be held. I often saw men in spats and high collars here, bank managers and their ilk. Most of the houses were so posh they had inside toilets. This is the area where Denis Healey, now Lord Healey of Riddlesden, used to live when a young boy in the 1920s. (Figure 4) His father had been appointed Principal of Keighley Technical School and the family had moved from south London. Lord Healey describes this area in his autobiography.

A stopping place on our walk home from school was Midland Terrace where we used to do our train spotting. Many of the big named expresses used this line in its heyday. It was a major route to Scotland. Midland Terrace, named after the Midland Railway Company, is overgrown now; and like so much of this area, is very run down. Incredible to think that fifty years ago some quite rich families lived here. The fine masonry on the well-built houses still points to that era. The railway was a great social boundary. A footbridge leads us to 'Lower Crustea', Lawkholme.

Lawkholme: Land of Snickets and Ginnels (Figure 5)

Lawkholme was an area of mills, iron foundries and heavy industry when I was a youth. The air used to be thick with purple smoke in fogbound winter and the men died early with mercury poisoning from an enamelling plant which was used here. During the winter vacations when I was at university I used to work in the Globe Ironworks maneouvering crucibles of molten iron for small moulds.

We wore clogs and leather shin guards. We used to work up such a thirst that the bar keeper in the Queen Street Arms, the original Grinning Rat, lined up a row of glasses of tepid water for us to down before we touched the beer. The beer was a strong mild brew. The first pint was free.

Most of the foundries are gone now. Where I worked in the town centre is just grass like the foundry yard here (Figure 7). Metal stamping and stocking manufacture were two other industries down the lane.

Not only the foundries, but also the church, Holy Trinity, has gone, as well as the Baptist church. For a dare we choirboys had to jump from a wall to a gas lamp-post in our cassock and

Figure 5. Lawkholme: land of ginnels and snickets.

Figure 6. A factory for sale. Lawkholme Lane.

Figure 7. Nature resurgent

surplice! I see there is just one tree left that I knew fifty years ago. By the time I reached the grammar school, it was my job to read the lessons at church, because I spoke 'proper'. The vicar here, when I was a boy, was The Reverend H.G.Wilks, a very radical churchman and thinker, and a great friend of J.M.Barrie. He named his three children, Peter, Michael and Wendy, after the characters in *Peter Pan*. They all went to local grammar schools. Sunday schools and church dances, with my Dad a bouncer, are vivid memories of what went on here, now a factory and a warehouse. (Figure 8)

Although it might not look it today, these houses were a cut above

Figure 8. 'Just a tree remains'. Lawkholme Lane.

Figure 9. Houses in Lawkholme Lane.

most of the others in the area. (Figure 9) They had a small frontage. Once they had iron railings, but these went towards the war effort in 1940. I was once painting the outside of the first floor window when I fell off. Jolly lucky I missed those railings, else I wouldn't be here now! There were three of us brothers, Harry, George and myself living in a terrace house like this with my sister, Rene, and our parents, and as Dad and we three lads were all over six foot, it was a very crowded house. We boys all went to the Grammar School and Leeds University, where we were the first three brothers to graduate. Much of our time was spent studying in the attic with our backs against the hot water cylinder, mittens and balaclavas on. We used to put slips of paper in pages as markers - no photocopying in those days - and I remember once mother tidying up the 'den' and pulling out all the slips! It took us days to put them all back.

It was a vibrant community and many of the adjacent houses were open house to us youngsters. There were gas lights in the houses opposite then, as well as in the street behind. Almost opposite our house was Tommy Holmes' Scrap Yard. It's still there today. One famous 'graduate' from Lawkholme is Keith Jessup, the wreck finder and salvage expert. I knew him well when young. He started in scrap iron, then did well recovering iron from the canal bed. In National Service he got training in diving, and the rest is history.

The street at the back of our house, more an alleyway, was Back Byrl Street. Two incidents here still amuse me. At one of the houses, the milkman's, Tom Pighills, we knocked an itinerant crow down his chimney with a shot from an air-gun my parents didn't know we had. The crow brought down a chimney-load of soot into their dining room just as the family were sitting down to tea. The air-gun was confiscated and we couldn't sit down for ages! Much later, when my brother and I were on leave from the army during National Service, we lobbed a snowball at a neighbour's door. It went straight through the glass pane! We sent a fiver anonymously through the post to cover breakage.

One job I had in my late teens was rent collecting for clients of my father. It meant visiting very run-down parts of the town, now all demolished, thank goodness.

Across from the end of our road was, and still is, the Rugby League ground. The Keighley team then was a great team. They had been to Wembley in 1937 and were very much the centre of our young lives. When watching, the generation before us used to sit on carts, and when we played and practised there, we changed at home and ran to the pitch already kitted up. Household names at that time were Freddie Barrett, Norman Foster, Joe Flanagan, Jack Mills, to name but a few.

Some of us from Lawkholme won scholarships to the grammar school and were bullied on our way home by the Jay Street Gang. They gave us a hard time and we came home the long way round through the Showfield area — until I learnt to box. This was at the Boxing Club behind the Grapes Inn. After that I was able to take the quickest way home from school down Lawkholme Lane and past the end of Parson Street, where we once ran the gauntlet of the Jay Street mob! (Figure 10) By the time I was in my mid-teens they left me well alone. Keith Jessop, who we met earlier, was one of the Jay Street Gang. In his book Gold Finder, he writes:

Figure 10. The 'Birdcage Area' of Parson Street.

Whenever I could, I escaped into the back streets of Lawkholme, in the Keighley district, with my gang of mates, the lads who lived in my very local area - the three streets surrounding my home. We called ourselves the Jay Street Gang. We felt like brothers and looked like them too, all dressed in shapeless, threadbare reach-me-downs and heavy boots or clogs, with our heads shaven like convicts. We played piggy-stick, kick-can, football and cricket, and in between times, we fought like cat and dog with other gangs in the vicinity.

Plover, Linnet, Nightingale, Thrush, Grouse, Wren, Pheasant, Hawk, Swallow and Quail Streets, streets known as the Bird Cage, still border Lawkholme and Parson Street today. My younger brother, George, had a boyhood scrap with Keith in Victoria Park. I don't know who won, but they became the best of friends afterwards.

The name on a sign is all that remains of our junior school, and that has been moved to a new first school built in Victoria Park. Clog fights, cricket and the Ton Weight game are three activities that remain clearly in mind. All were played in the old playground. Wickets were chalked on the factory wall. Ton Weight was a rather rough game in which two teams of boys on each other's shoulders fought to shift the other team's jockey. Skating down long icy slides in winter was another favourite past-time for boys. Girls had many skipping games and sang catches as they skipped. Kendall Mellor, the Channel swimmer, was a contemporary of mine at Eastwood School. Another pupil, Joan Smith, was a contemporary here of my sister (who later taught here). Joan Smith is better known as the 1950s film starlet, Sandra Dawn, who achieved international fame and starred in short parts in Hollywood films. She was so beautiful that Jacob Epstein cast a bronze bust of her. This stands in London's

Figure 11. The Mansion House.

Figure 12. Emily Street, the boyhood home of Lord Briggs.

Royal Festival Hall. Miss Boase was one headmistress in my time. She had been a pupil of Tolkien at university.

The Mansion House, now a leisure centre, was Keighley's first museum. (Figure 11) Keighley was full of wealthy industrialists who shared the Victorian rich man's mania for collecting. And not only rich people. My family were fairly poor, but we gave things to the Museum. Everybody did. The Museum was full of specimens, instruments, costumes, lichens, mummies. It was our university.

> *The Museum was one great treasure-house. Not an inch was wasted. Narrow aisles ran between close-packed cases and cabinets; from the walls above hung flags and halberds, animals' heads and caught fishes of record sizes. From frozen kingfishers and golden eagles eternally feeding their young you turned to old fire-engines or Great War revolvers; geology rubbed shoulders with military uniforms, Egyptology with autographs of the famous. (*Ian Dewhirst. You Don't Remember Bananas ...)*

The Egyptian mummy I remember well. When it got dark, the museum was very spooky and our imaginations played riot. The curators, Maurice Longbottom and John Ogden were enlightened people. One lad who studied here all hours, escaping from an over-crowded house in Emily Street, was Asa Briggs, later Professor Asa Briggs, now Lord Briggs of Lewes. (Figure 12) As school children in the 1940s, we were brought to the museum by Miss Lambert from Eastwood School, just over the way, to study the history and natural

Figure 13. Keighley Station

history of the area through well-displayed exhibits. Facing the Mansion House, then, as now, is Victoria Park. This used to be the scene of boxing matches at the annual Gala, run to raise money for the local Victoria Hospital. I once won fifty 'ciggies' here.

For three years I commuted daily to Leeds. As undergraduates living less than thirty miles from Leeds, my two brothers and I had to live at home. I also have memories of waiting at the station, like many Keighley servicemen catching and leaving trains here when coming and going off leave. (Figure 13) Often I'd arrive on leave in the early hours of the morning having caught the 'milk train' from Leeds. Army greatcoats were especially valued when there was no heat in the trains during the winter of 1955. It's nice to see steam engines still in use here as they chug up the Worth Valley to Oakworth, Haworth and Oxenhope.

The Town

Cavendish Street is one of Keighley's glories, but 'hidden' high above the heads of the busy shoppers is Gordon Bottomley's plaque. Why is it, I wonder, that we don't celebrate our famous sons and daughters more? Dr Gordon Bottomley was an outstanding poet and editor of his time. He befriended a whole host of Georgian poets such as Robert Frost, Edward Thomas, Laurence Binyon and John Drinkwater. Where are the plaques to the historians Herbert

Butterfield and Asa Briggs? Or to politicians like Philip Snowden and Denis Healey? Or to artists Alex Smith and Hildred Harpin, my old teacher at the Grammar School. He painted many murals in mid-Wales churches after he'd become a Roman Catholic parish priest down there. He died in Assissi where he'd retired as an old man to be a chaplain at the great cathedral. Hildred was a great inspirer. So was my old English teacher, Kenneth Preston. Actress Sandra Dawn and dear Mollie Sugden, another local girl, also deserve permanent celebration.

Opposite Gordon Bottomley's plaque is the Cycling Club. (Figure 14) My father was a life member of the Cycling Club, and so am I. This club can tell some tales! It is one of the oldest clubs in Keighley. There is the story of the lion. A circus was visiting Keighley Hippodrome, the local theatre just across the road from the club (demolished in the 1960s). One of the acts was a lion who did tricks. On asking the lion tamer over for a drink at the club, he asked my father if the lion could come too! 'He is very well behaved' said the keeper. So in they all went, up the stairs, lion as well, and through the swing doors at the top. A number of members were drinking noisily in the club - until they saw the lion. They all went quiet for a minute, then, in a flash, they jumped over the bar and pulled down the grille. The lion was frightened and jumped on the billiard table, where, in its fright, it peed all over the table, which was ruined! My father was banned from the club till he'd paid for the table's re-covering.

Another story related to the escapologist, Harry Houdini. After a few pints he was persuaded to cycle round the block blindfolded. And thoroughly blindfolded he was too. Some plaster stuff was put

Figure 14. The Cycling Club, Cavendish Street.

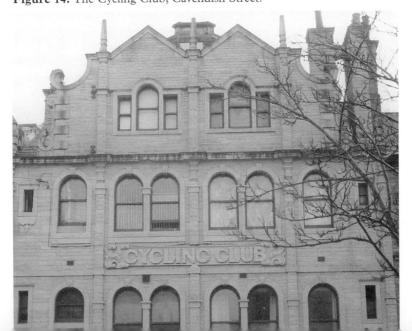

Figure 15. The War Memorial.

over his eyes, then bound over several times. There was no way he could see anything. And do you know, cycle round the block he did! He didn't have to pay for a drink the whole time he was in Keighley.

My father and elder brother Harry served in the forces and lost many friends in the war, friends they grew up with. My father served in both the First and Second World Wars, in the Royal Flying Corps, and the Royal Air Force. He was forty when he volunteered for the Second World War in which he was injured. My brother served in the Royal Navy. The war memorial is a fine tribute to the fallen from both World Wars. (Figure 15). On a lighter note, there's a story, apocryphal I'm sure, that the sailor with the spy glass was looking directly at a ladies toilet. The toilet was moved! On the other side of the memorial the soldier has lost the bayonet from his rifle. It was removed by Bradford Council to stop vandals bayonetting themselves when climbing around the Memorial, though I believe a removable wooden lookalike is inserted for civic occasions.

I had an uncle, Harry Waddington Feather, who was a sidesman at the Parish Church here and at Ingrow Parish Church, which was built by my great-great-grandfather, Joshua Waddington. (Figure 16).

My grandfather, Luke Feather, was innkeeper at the *Great Northern Inn* next to Ingrow Parish Church. The inn and the church came from the same quarry, I believe, and Grandfather Luke married Joshua Waddington's granddaughter, Ada. So as an Anglican priest, I have a foot in both pulpit and pub. Both the Feathers and the Waddingtons migrated down the Worth Valley from Haworth in the 1840s when Ingrow was beginning to be built. My great grandfather, William Feather, was, in fact, baptised by Patrick Brontë.

Keighley's streets hold fond memories of shopping on Saturday mornings for my mother, who worked in the mill till mid-day on Saturdays during the war and shortly after. (Figures 17, 18) Our butcher was near Temple Row, up High Street. His name was Jimmy Lever and he was a great patron of the Queen's Theatre, demolished in 1961. He had autographed photographs and cartoons of various well known comics like George Formby, framed and hung in his butcher's shop. He always wore a bowler hat in the shop with his butcher's apron. I went shopping armed with a ration book and generally finished up at the Milk Bar in Lawkholme Crescent.

Like Keighley's museum, the public library was, and still is, one of Keighley's glories. (Figure 19). It was the first public library in England to be funded by the Scottish-American philanthropist, Andrew Carnegie. It is also a rare example in the north of England of the Arts and Craft style of architecture that owed its inspiration to William Morris. I spent many long hours here, in the 'people's

Figure 16. The Parish Church.

Figure 17. The Royal Arcade.

Figure 18. Jean City.

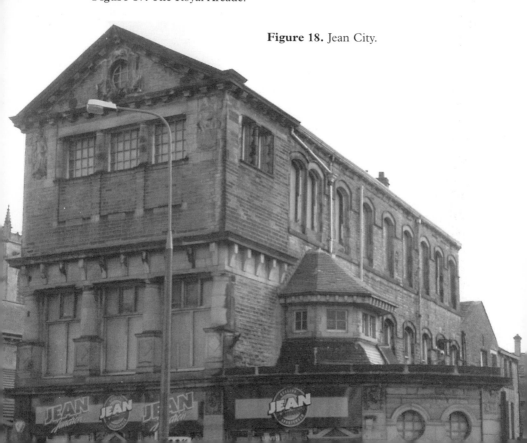

Figure 19. The 'Carnegie' Public Library.

university'. It is another reason why Keighley produced so many famous scholars. And not just scholars. Goldfinder Keith Jessop was the son of a penniless mill-girl, who left school without a single qualification. Keighley was, as he himself writes, the least likely of places to start such a lucrative career:

> *It is about as far from the sea as you can get in northern England....*
> *One typically grey and wet Keighley afternoon, I and my mates were*
> *whiling away the time in the public library when I came across a*
> *picture book about famous shipwrecks and the treasures lost with*
> *them.*

He sat 'spellbound' and later 'With the help of patient librarians in the public libraries in Bradford, Keighley and further afield, I read every book and article about shipwrecks I could get my hands on.'

Gone alas, is the magnificent Victorian Mechanics' Institute building. (Figure 20) The 1960s-built Keighley Technical College is there now. The Institute used to have a fine clock tower, a miniature of Big Ben. We boys from the Grammar School, which was part of

Figure 20. The Mechanics' Institute. *Bradford City Libraries*

the Institute, used to have a 'smokers' union' in the roof of the Institute below the clock tower. One day, one of the lads pulled a lever, and the hour bell rang, and rang, and rang! We scarpered! The Institute was burnt down in 1962 after a fire following the Saturday night dance. Keighley lost both its Grammar Schools (now comprehensives) and the town's focal point in the 1960s. A frequent visitor to Keighley was the novelist G.K.Chesterton, who came to lecture. It was here that he met Father O'Connor, who was the model for his detective Father Brown.

The Temperance Hall is another fine example of Victorian architecture. (Figure 21) I remember attending meetings of the Keighley Natural History, Literary and Debating Society which were held there. In winter, there was a full lecture programme illustrated with lantern slides. In summer we went on long rambles over the nearby moors and dales. John Ogden, the museum curator, was the driving force behind it when I was a boy.

Once Keighley had six or more cinemas. The Ritz was a beautiful 1930s cinema complete with Wurlitzer. It was played for a time by Stanley Bishop, who was also our church organist. The cinemas were a glorious escape into fantasy. Gene Autrey was our favourite star as

Figure 21. The Temperance Hall.

boys. Once we were playing in a field just below the cricket field. We had seen that film where Gene Autrey dropped from a tree straight onto the back of a horse. 'I dare you' said Tommy Barritt to my brother. My brother George dared, and dropped down onto a the back of a cart-horse. Normally a placid horse which we know well, he shot off, dismounting my brother in the process and jumped the wall. He then galloped across the newly shorn and immaculately rolled cricket square, and eventually came to halt somewhere up Lawkholme Lane. My father had to pay for a lot a damage! Many years later, and after a distinguished army career, the instigator of this dare became one of Keighley's policemen. In earlier days in Keighley you had to 'win your spurs' as a policeman by fighting. Only after you had acquitted yourself well in a fight with local toughies were you accorded respect by those you had to police. But that was before the war. Things changed somewhat in war-time when most able-bodied men were in the forces.

One snowy afternoon I was in town with some of my Catholic friends. Across North Street was St. Anne's Roman Catholic Church

Figure 22. The Virgin Mary, Skipton Road.

and school. High up on the front was a statue of the Virgin Mary . (Figure 22) 'Can you,' asked Peter O'Connell, 'hit that statue with a snowball?' 'Of course I can' I said, and did. 'Fluke!' said another friend. So I hit it again. Five or six times in all. Then, out of the convent next door appeared an angry young nun, complete in black habit and hood. My friends evaporated and I took off like greased lightning, scarpering along Skipton Road. The nun, Sister Monica, chased me. Could she run! She chased me all the way home and wouldn't leave till my father had given me a thrashing.

We finish our walk back at the tea room at Cliffe Castle Museum. Foundries, parks, lions, shipwrecks,rugby, stuffed owls, Sister Monica and the Jay Street Gang: what an amazing place this Keighley is! The photographs, bar one, are mine, but the memories are John's, plus a few from Lord Healey, Keith Jessop and Ian Dewhirst. My thanks to them all and to their publishers, Penguin Books, Simon and Shuster, and The Ridings Publishing Company. Editor.

Sources

Ian Dewhirst *You don't remember bananas: a Pennine half-century,* The Ridings Publishing Company, 1985.
Denis Healey *The Time of My Life*, Penguin,1989.
Keith Jessop *Goldfinder*. Simon & Shuster, 1998.

Further Reading
J. Stuart Cardwell *Keighley: a pictorial history*. Phillimore,1997
Ian Dewhirst *A history of Keighley*. Keighley Corporation, 1974
Ian Dewhirst *Images of Keighley*. Breedon Books, 1996
Ian Dewhirst *Keighley in the 1930s & 1940s*. Hendon Publishing Co.,1989
John Waddington-Feather *Garlic Lane* 2nd ed., Feather Books, 1998

11. SALTAIRE – VISION TO VISION

by Clive Woods

TITUS SALT, ONE OF EIGHT CHILDREN, was born at Morley near Leeds, on the 20th September 1803. He died on the 29th December 1876, leaving behind a textile empire the like of which had never been seen before. At first, Salt wanted to be a doctor, but the sight of blood made him faint, so doctoring was not for Titus. Instead he became a woolstapler, buying and selling wool, and with his father, Daniel, developed the firm of Daniel Salt and Son into one of the most successful wool businesses in Bradford and the world.

Six foot tall, with black hair, Titus Salt was a good looking man, serious, but very inventive (Figure 1). His knowledge of wool production enabled him to forsee that alpaca wool he found abandoned in a warehouse in Liverpool could be commercially spun. The alpaca is a member of the camel family and is found in Peru and Chile. Salt spun the fibre which gave the quality of silk for the price of wool. He created a new staple and made a fortune. (Figure 2)

Figure 1. Sir Titus Salt.
Saltaire Tourist Information Centre

Instead of retiring and cashing in on his inventiveness, Salt, at the age of 48, started to build Saltaire in the rural Aire Valley as an answer to the problems created by industrialisation in the mid-Victorian era. Saltaire was not just a social vision, but an industrial one as well. The nature of the man meant that he grasped the current thinking on sanitation, health, welfare, mass production and safety at work. He tested his theories and proved his solutions.

Built on the banks of the river Aire, Saltaire had the infrastructure

Figure 2. Alpacas from Penrith. *Bernard Hibbert*

for what was to become the greatest Victorian industrial experiment. In the 1850s Salt was operating an integrated transport policy for his industrial exploits: alpaca from Liverpool via the Leeds-Liverpool canal to feed 1,200 looms producing seventeen miles of cloth a day, to be transported by rail to the port of Hull and onto Europe and the world. Salt created mass production long before Henry Ford and was one of the first men to foresee the role of railways in the development of an industry. But mass production had a price, and Salt's price was a contract between himself and his workforce. His workers would produce high quality cloth in as safe an environment as he could create. In return he would grasp the nettles of bad housing, non-existing sanitation and poor health.

Nineteenth century wooltowns were attracting thousands of country people to appalling living conditions and an early death. Life expectancies in the 1840s Bradford was 20 years and 3 months, about 50 if you discount the 0 to 5 year old deaths. Salt was taking his workers back home to the countryside. Within twenty five years he had created his vision. Each house had its own privy and water supply. Saltaire had the world's first modern launderette, with centrifugal spinners and hot air blowers. The Victoria Hall was

Figure 3. George Street, Saltaire, c.1900. *Saltaire Village Society*

provided for recreation with library, reading room, billiard room, concert hall, gym and, typical of the inventive Salt, a science lab. It wasn't free, costing men over 21 six shillings per quarter, and women and children three shillings. A school was provided in 1868 before the Forster Education Act of 1870, to give a sound education. Anyone becoming destitute, if of good character, could live in an armshouse, rent free, and with a pension equal to an unskilled worker's wage at the mill. In the 1860s, Salt developed a sickness benefit scheme and provided a hospital. A church and a park met the spiritual and physical welfare of his workforce. By the time of his death in 1876, the vision was complete. He was brought home to Saltaire and laid to rest in his church next to the mill. But the Salt family did not prosper for long on the fruits of the father. The family fortunes were served a disastrous blow when Salt's successor, Titus junior, died in 1887 at the age of 44. By 1892 the family had sold the mill and village. New industrialists like James Roberts moved in and Saltaire settled down to becoming a mill town. (Figure 3)

By 1933 the housing needed major repairs and the millowners did not want to pay the bill. The houses were sold to the Bradford Property Trust Ltd and Saltaire was sold off with most of the houses becoming owner occupied.

With the slow decline of the British wool industry, the fortunes of the mill slumped. By the 1980s the New Mill, added on the north bank of the canal in 1868, was totally derelict. Victoria Hall and the school, structurally unsafe, were closed. A body-blow came in the form of the Department of Transport, West Yorkshire County Council and Bradford Metropolitan District Council who wanted four lanes of highway through the park in the form of a 'cut-and-cover' tunnel. As Reg Atkinson, Bradford's Director of Development Services told Yorkshire Television in 1985, 'At the end of the day the little man has to move to make way for progess.'

In February 1986, Illingworth Morris closed the original mill. Saltaire was well and truly on the skids. House prices were plummeting and it looked as if the future was dereliction and possible annihilation. Salt's dream had hit rock bottom.

The size of the houses in Saltaire had created a peculiar problem. Most houses were either two-up two-down or two-down three-up. This meant that the houses were attractive to young couples without a family. With the birth of two or three children, they became crowded and most couples moved out. The housing was also attractive to the elderly - cheap, easy to maintain and heat. Neither the elderly nor young couples make the best fighters in a cause where national and local government has to be taken on.

Without knowing it, there was one glimmer of light. The housing no longer depended on the fortunes of the mill. On 8 April 1984, the railway station, closed in the 1960s, was re-opened. Saltaire was suddenly ten minutes from Bradford, twenty minutes from Leeds, and three hours from London. (Figure 4) You could have a house in the countryside, facing the moors, and commute to the city. Saltaire housing began to look attractive to professional people without a family. The invasion of the professionals, with jobs and money to spend on housing, started as a trickle soon to become a flood. With this change in population, more articulate people moved in who knew how to present an argument and how to put a spanner in the works of government.

In 1984 the nouveau Saltaire residents, with interested locals, banded together to form the Saltaire Village Society to fight the road scheme through the park, and start to battle for Saltaire. The village had a voice and no opportunity was lost in making that voice heard. Since the houses are compact and neighbours know each other,

Figure 4. Albert Terrace, Saltaire. Photograph by Jonathan Silver. *Salts Estates*

strangers are very noticeable. Strangers with notebooks and pens set alarm bells off. Such a stranger appeared in 1985, an architect working for English Heritage thinking of Listing the end houses of the streets. The Village Society pounced, hijacked the architect to a cafe and refused to let him go until he had heard their views. Saltaire in parts meant little, but as a whole it was of major industrial and architectual importance. List the whole, not the parts. After the third cup of coffee and the second cream cake, the case was won, and within four days the Village was listed for the nation. Reg Atkinson of Bradford City Hall began to realise the 'little man' had cunning, guile and teeth!

The Aire Valley Trunk Road is the longest ongoing pulic inquiry in the history of road building in Britain. This has created a large group of people who understand the workings of public enquiries and how

Figure 5. Lord Mayor's Victorian Funday, June 1985. *Larry Anderson*

to influence an Inspector at such an inquiry. The Village Society joined together with other anti-road groups, and under the name of the Aire Valley Joint Road Committee began to lobby for alternative routes to the valley bottom through Saltaire.

By 1990 the Committee had convinced a third public inquiry to ditch the road through the park. Using the media, the Village Society used every opportunity to promote Saltaire as an ideal place to live and of its major importance in the industrial heritage of Britain and the world.

In the late 1980s the national attitude to Victorian architecture was changing and various planning officers, who had helped to mutilate Victorian Bradford, had retired. The planning environment was changing. People were looking to find alternative uses for large buildings, and Saltaire had plenty of big buildings. The first move in this direction came in 1985, when Pam and Phil Fluke brought their world famous collection of reed organs and harmoniums to Victoria Hall and started a centre of excellence in the village. But still the two mills were empty and one was derelict.

As if by magic a new Salt arrived. Jonathan Silver had made his money out of clothing shops. In 1979 he sold his thirteen shops and by 1983 was in partnership with Sir Ernest Hall at Dean Clough Mill in Halifax. By 1985 he had sold out to Hall and gone on a world tour with his family. 1986 saw him looking for a new project and on 10 June 1987, Salt's Mill was chosen.

At the start Silver bewildered the locals when the first thing he did was to put on

Figure 6. David Hockney at work. Photograph by Jonathan Silver. *Salts Estate*

a production of West Side Story with Opera North. What was the man doing?

Silver was always on the move. He was an approachable person who did not hide in an office behind secretaries. His door was always open - if you could find which door! To make him happy all you had to do was to set up three separate meetings in the same room while he was using two telephones at the same time, as well as arguing with a roofer over a job estimate. Blink, and he was gone. Sneeze, and he would have clinched a deal in America. When Silver got an idea in his head he was relentless until it was successful or needed to be abandoned. While serving in the bar during West Side Story he had the idea of creating an international art gallery dedicated to the work of his friend David Hockney. Initially Hockney was very wary of the idea and did not visit the gallery for eighteen months. When he eventually came he liked what he saw and the David and Jonathan show began (Figures 6 and 7).

World premiers were held in Saltaire, not London. They forced the art world out of the capital to Saltaire. In fact, the premier of the Yorkshire Landscapes started in Saltaire, went to Boston (USA),

Figure 7. David Hockney and Jonathan Silver. *Salts Estate*

Figure 8. Saltaire roof tops. Photograph by Jonathan Silver. *Salts Estate*

then Paris, and finally Bonn, where it was sold off. The international art world suddenly saw Saltaire as one of its centres and the heritage of the village was given a new slant.

As Salt had seen the wealth potential of Alpaca, so Silver saw that microtechnology, and one of the largest mills in the world, had a lot in common. He realised that firms needed space, lots of space. They needed to be able to expand and contract at the drop of a hat. One thing Salt's mill had in abundance was space, eight hundred thousand square feet of it.

In 1990 Silver signed up with Pace Microtechnology as a major user of the mill. By 1996 he had sold land to another microtechnology firm, Filtronic Comtek, and a new factory emerged built of stone with a slate roof in keeping with the village. Now the vision was in place: high technology and the arts, with high technology paying for the arts. The results of such vision was a regeneration which helped the conservation of the village.

The sight of the mill beginning to flourish again was a major

incentive for Bradford Council to enter into a partnership with English Heritage. A Town Scheme was established in 1989 where 40% grants were offered to the villagers to re-instate original fixtures and fittings. Between 1989 and March 1998 the Council and English Heritage had put £635,000 into the Town Scheme and the villagers £952,000: a total of just over one and a half million pounds, or £19,000 per house. (Figure 8) Saltaire was becoming confident and bullish, proud of its history and the new direction it was taking. With the success of the original mill, the New Mill across the canal became an attractive prospect. Property developers gazumped Silver, bought the New Mill, and found a major user in the Bradford Area Health Authority. The New Mill owes its survival to Titus Salt, who had made it fireproof and able to withstand anything you could throw at it. For over twenty years it had stood derelict and open to the elements. But when work started on its refurbishment all it needed was re-pointing, re-roofing, and new fixtures and fittings. A 'brand new' Victorian mill arose on the doorsteps of Bradford, Leeds and Keighley. (Figure 9)

People were now wanting housing in Saltaire, so it was obvious that the canal and riverside sections of the New Mill would make ideal flats. Within a short time all the flats were sold. Saltaire was on the up and up. Money was found to refurbish Victoria Hall and the old school became part of Shipley College. Saltaire had become a vibrant busy place and with its success came recognition. In 1996 Saltaire won the top Civic Trust Award, the Centre Vision Award, and also a top European Award, the Europa Nostra Medal. 1997 brought recognition from the British Urban Regeneration Association, one of five schemes selected out of forty. The church saw

Figure 9. The refurbished New Mill. *Bradford Heritage Recording Unit*

restoration work begin in 1998 and when this is complete Saltaire
will be up and running for at least another hundred years.

The success of Silver's vision also attracted more retail into the
Mill and Victoria Road. The Mill offered art, books, furnishings,
clothing, designer products for the home, and a diner. Victoria Road
provided three secondhand bookshops, two art galleries, a huge
antique centre with books, and places to eat. The Victoria Hall was
in demand for musical concerts and in 1999 will headline Cherish
the Ladies, Julie Felix, Isla St Claire and Lindisfarne. Saltaire has
become a place to visit, to shop, appreciate art, and buy books. It

now has its own Tourist Information Centre. 1999 saw the Government nominate the village for World Heritage status, the greatest accolade so far.

Why has regeneration in Saltaire been a success while elsewhere schemes have collapsed? The answer lies in the vision of two men. Titus Salt and Jonathan Silver were at the cutting edge of the technologies of their day. Salt built for the future. His housing is still comfortable to live in today and is much sought after. Silver had the vision to see the potential re-use of one of the biggest mills in the world. The people of Saltaire owe a deep debt of gratitude to the inventiveness of Salt and Silver. Both were men who didn't let obstacles get in their way. Both had a vision each wanted to make a reality. Today Saltaire is an excellent example of how history can be kept alive by diversification. Saltaire has come full circle, but not without tragedy. On Thursday 25 September 1997, at the age of 47, Jonathan Silver died of cancer. Fortunately for Saltaire, his death, unlike that of Titus Salt junior, was not sudden and Jonathan was able to provide for the future of the mill. In only ten years he helped to regenerate Saltaire. Salt and Silver are synonymous with vision and success. It has been a pleasure observing both men at work.

Further Reading

Jim Greenhalf *Salt & Silver: a story of hope* 2nd ed., Bradford Libraries, 1998
Jack Reynolds *The great paternalist: Titus Salt and the growth of nineteenth century Bradford.* Temple Smith, 1983
Jack Reynolds *Saltaire: an introduction to the village of Sir Titus Salt.* 1985
R. Balgarnie *Sir Titus Salt, Baronet: his life and its lessons.* London, 1877
A. Holroyd *Saltaire and its Founder, Sir Titus Salt, Bart.* Bradford, 1873

12. FAVOURITE HAUNTS AND HIDDEN CORNERS: A PHOTOGRAPHER'S VIEW OF BRADFORD

by Richard Newman

IF WE WERE TO VIEW a tourist's snapshots from their visit to Bradford, what would we see? Probably the City Hall, certainly the National Museum of Photography, Film and Television and very likely one or two images of Cartwright Hall and Salts Mill, where a varied selection of David Hockney's artwork is permanently on display. But what about the other Bradford? The lesser-known buildings and the hidden corners which are equally as interesting as their more famous brothers and sisters?

One of my personal favourite haunts, which is quite close to where I live, is Undercliffe Cemetery. It contains so much of the city's history and is so very atmospheric. It also houses one of the finest collections of Victorian funerary art in the country and, not surprisingly, is visited by people from all over the world.

The view over the city from the western end of the Central Promenade is without doubt quite spectacular but when it is also enhanced by a breathtakingly beautiful Turneresque skyscape of oranges, yellows, pinks and gold it is truly magnificent. I witnessed such a sky with my friend Alexis about twelve years ago. We stood there late one winter afternoon with our heads and necks craned back admiring the huge multi-coloured canopy of colour-tinged clouds above us. It spread far and wide over the bowl of Bradford and beyond. It was absolutely amazing and unforgettable. I have seen many wonderful open skies and beautiful sunsets there since, but none quite as stunning as on that memorable occasion.

I love the way that dramatic light can transform a landscape or subject. In fact quality of light is very important to me and I especially like bright winter and spring days when the low sun casts long shadows (Figure 1).

I also enjoy working when the light is beginning to fade and the subjects gradually silhouette against a slowly darkening sky (Figure 2).

Bradford has such a wonderfully hilly landscape (Figure 3) though I doubt many cyclists or OAP's would agree. In fact, John Schlesinger, the famous film director, said recently that he chose

Figure 1. Winter Shadows. Undercliffe Cemetery. *Richard Newman*

Figure 2. Dimming of the Day. Undercliffe Cemetery. *Richard Newman*

Figure 3. A Steep Climb. Terraced housing near Peel Park. *Richard Newman*

Bradford as the location for the film Billy Liar because of all the hills and also because of the huge redevelopment that was taking place in the city centre in the early 1960s.

I was wandering around near Peel Park with my camera one day when I spotted the rather unusual sight of two pairs of trousers drying in the sun, each pair in a separate window (Figure 4). I love

Figure 4. Totally Legless. *Richard Newman*

Figure 5. Striking a Pose. Second Hand Shop, Low Moor. *Richard Newman*

quirky subjects like this, unfortunately they are all too rare. However, driving through Low Moor to visit friends one night, my girlfriend spotted a strange figure in a shop window (Figure 5). On the way home I stopped the car to take a closer look. Such was my enthusiasm that I returned first thing the next morning praying on the way that it would still be there; thankfully it was. However, the shrewd junk shop owner unbelievably tried to extract money from me for the privilege of taking some photographs. It was only when his partner intervened and told him to leave me alone that he eased off. When I'd finished he invited me into his 'spiders web' (shop) to look around. The same man that had tried to extract money from me now did his level best to sell me a huge glass fish that he insisted would look 'nice' in my home. I left empty-handed a few minutes later.

The Bradford district is graced by several fine railway viaducts; arguably the two most impressive are Hewenden Viaduct near Harecroft and Thornton Viaduct on Alderscholes Lane (Figure 6). Another that I always greatly admired but which has since been demolished, was the one near Wyke and Norwood Green (Figure 7). It cut across the valley beautifully. Luckily though, I managed to capture it one cold and frosty morning a couple of years before it was dynamited.

Queensbury was once a busy triangular-shaped railway junction with trains to Bradford, Halifax and Keighley. You certainly wouldn't think so if you visited the site today. There are very few remnants left.

Figure 6. Thornton Viaduct. *Richard Newman*

Figure 7. Frosty Morning. Viaduct near Wyke and Norwood Green. *Richard Newman*

Figure 8. Is There Anybody There?, Queensbury Station. *Richard Newman*

However, the station master's house is still there and an old rusting metal overbridge (Figure 8). I walked around the area with my camera about six years ago and was very surprised to find a subway, a couple of overgrown platforms and even a huge concrete Queensbury Station nameboard. There was also a small very attractive stone viaduct. After I had inspected all of the remains I walked along the cutting towards Clayton tunnel. I then stopped underneath the old metal overbridge, the pin-holed smoke deflectors above fascinating me; rusting remnants from the days of steam locomotives.

I always think that this photograph (Figure 8) has a very sinister feel to it. One almost expects there to be a 'mad axeman' lurking somewhere in the shadows.

Forster Square Station is fortunately still very much in service and well used. A far cry however from when this photograph (Figure 9) was taken in the early 1990s shortly before demolition of the old buildings and platforms. The gypsy horse was one of several tethered in between the platforms on the old track beds.

There are few mill chimneys left in Bradford today. It was a very different situation though fifty or a hundred years ago when a forest of them belched smoke out onto the city blackening the buildings and no doubt the local population's lungs at the same time. It is strange how we become nostalgic about things when they start to disappear, and even more peculiar when one realises what a health hazard they were.

I suddenly realised in 1984 that the mills and their chimneys were

Figure 9. The Horse Now Standing. Forster Square Station, Bradford. *Richard Newman*

Figure 10. Industrial Landscape, Bradford 1984. *Richard Newman*

vanishing from the Bradford landscape at an alarming rate (Figure 10). This was of course partly due to closure and demolition but also to the numerous mill fires that were occurring with suspicious regularity. I think that I just managed to catch a glimpse of the Old Bradford before it changed completely.

One of Bradford's best-known landmarks is Lister's Mill chimney (Figure 11), viewed from Bolton Woods.

Pictured (Figure 12) is another fine chimney constructed of brick, which has survived on borrowed time for some years now. I decided that I must photograph it before it vanished from the landscape

Figure 11. Listers Mill from Bolton Woods. *Richard Newman*

forever. The huge white cloud in the photograph was moving rapidly into the frame as I focussed. Just then a group of inquisitive and very distracting children arrived on the scene. 'Wot you tekkin a picture of mister? Is it gonna be in the newspaper? You're tekkin a picture of the chimney?, why, is it gonna be knocked down?' Meanwhile the

Figure 12. Head in the Clouds, lone chimney, Barkerend. *Richard Newman*

cloud, a cracking one at that, had almost escaped me, but not quite, thankfully.

Some time ago I watched the film *Life at the Top* which was of course the sequel to John Braine's *Room at the Top*. The opening and closing shots of the film were taken through a very ornate pair of wrought iron mill gates. Regrettably, these have now gone but a small section of fence remains (Figure 13) which is similar in style to the missing gates.

This conservatory in Bradford Moor Park was awaiting demolition when I photographed it. I climbed in through a gap in the surrounding chestnut paling

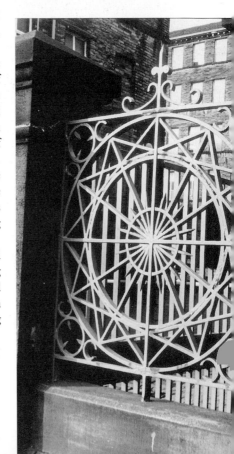

Figure 13. A Star In It's Own Right. Thornton Road. *Richard Newman*

Figure 14. The Greenhouse Effect. Bradford Moor Park. *Richard Newman*

Figure 15. Old Doorway. Boy and Barrel Public House, City Centre. *Richard Newman*

and crunched my way over a carpet of broken glass. I looked up to admire the beautiful decorative cast iron roof spandrels and columns. Suddenly the sun came out from behind a cloud; it illuminated the whole scene perfectly, it's final moment of glory captured on film (Figure 14).

   This lovely old doorway (Figure 15) with it's decorative surround and stained glass window caught my eye a few years ago. It was

Figure 16. Grotesque, Old Empire Theatre Entrance, Great Horton Road.
Richard Newman

obviously well used at one time judging by the wear on the step. I'll bet that it could tell a few tales! But one just wonders why it was blocked up in the first place.

This little chap (Figure 16) was still smiling away to himself, even though his days were numbered in October 1993. He was, in fact, surrounded by scaffolding; the Alexandra hotel was being demolished. For many years however, he had greeted Empire Theatre and Cinema-goers as they entered the building. He was just one of a collection of grotesques which adorned the stucco columns of the frontage. The auditorium was actually at the rear of the building and the entrance was through the hotel. It originally opened as a music hall at the end of the last century. Many famous entertainers appeared here over the years including Charlie Chaplin,

Figure 17. End Of The Empire. Old Empire Theatre/Alexandra Hotel during demolition. *Richard Newman*

Harry Houdini and WC Fields. Bradford author J B Priestley was a regular visitor to the Empire Music Hall and spent many happy hours there in his youth watching the performances. From 1972 up until the early 1990s the Alex was owned by Bradford College and used as an annexe. The demolished building (Figure 17) – which was brick and stucco, not stone – was tipped into the disused railway cutting approaching Well Heads Tunnel at Thornton.

This rather interesting structure (Figure 18) with it's protruding gargoyles was situated at the top of Manor Row on Manningham

Figure 18. The clock-tower, Old Bradford Boys Grammar School, Manningham Lane. *Richard Newman*

Figure 19. The Nurseries, Six-Days-Only, Heaton. *Richard Newman*

Figure 20. Hartley and May Gudgeon, Six-Days-Only, Heaton. *Richard Newman*

Lane. It was originally part of the old Bradford Boys Grammar School but in later years was used by Carlton Boys Grammar. Sadly it was demolished in 1987.

The countryside is still surprisingly close to Bradford City Centre. An area that I am especially fond of is Heaton Woods and the little hamlet known as Six-Days-Only (Figure 19) perhaps best known for the sale of Nettle Beer. The local newspapers have speculated for years about the place name but were never quite sure of its origin. In 1991 I photographed and interviewed William Hartley Gudgeon who had been a nurseryman there for over 60 years (Figure 20). Hartley, as he was more commonly known, moved to Six-Days-Only when he was 19 years old and told me: 'everything wa wild when we came 'ere. There wa no water, you ad to fetch it with a bucket from the woods. I've been ere sixty some years, time passes on dunt it' he beamed. 'You know I used to grow roses by the thousand at one time, and I had a hen run.'

The name, Six-Days-Only, Hartley told me, originated from the time when a Salvation Army man rented the nurseries. 'He wa reet religious and he wouldn't open up on a Sunday'. The Salvation Army man constructed a sign in the shape of a cross, made from old floorboards, it was painted white with black letters, 'only' was written across and 'six-days' down. 'Somebody tried to buy the old floorboards sign after he'd left' Hartley told me. 'But it were too late, we'd broken it up and used it as firewood!' Sadly Hartley Gudgeon died in November 1997. His wife moved out of the house but still lives in the Heaton area.

CONTRIBUTORS

Bob Duckett was born in South Wales and grew up in Enfield and Croydon. He came to Bradford during the 1974 local government re-organisation via Glasgow, Leicester, Bangor (North Wales) and Birmingham. He was appointed Reference Librarian in 1985. As well as being active in professional affairs, Bob has been responsible for Bradford Libraries' publishing programme where he has seen through the press some thirty books on local history. As well as being the editor of the *Transactions* of the Brontë Society, Bob has just accepted the post of editor of the *Bradford Antiquary*. He is a Fellow of the Library Association, an MA, and is currently writing a chapter for the *Cambridge History of Libraries of the British Isles*.

1. LAW AND DISORDER IN MEDIEVAL BRADFORD

Geoffrey Greenhough was brought up in Low Moor and Wyke, and educated at Bradford Grammar School and Sheffield University. He joined the RAF as an education officer, serving sixteen years and retiring in the rank of Squadron Leader. He then attended theological college and was ordained in the Church of England in 1975. He is currently vicar of Pott Shrigley, a small village in the Cheshire Peak District. A member of the Bradford Family History Society, he has always fostered a keen interest in local history. Geoffrey and his wife Irene have four children and ten grandchildren.

2. THE TRAGEDY OF JERRY DELANEY: HERO OF THE BROOMFIELDS

Ronnie Wharton is a life-long enthusiast of folk music and sport, an enthusiasm which has found expression in publications such as *The Crown Street Comic Band* (1977) and The *Tommy Talker Bands of the West Riding* (1979), both with Arthur Clarke, and *The Best of Bradford Amateur Football* (1987) and *The Pick of Bradford Amateur Football* (1987). Much of the material has found its way into the feature columns of local papers throughout Yorkshire. Ronnie currently writes a regular column on the local football scene in the Yorkshire Sports. His other occupation is a clerk in the textile trade.

3. THORNTON VILLAGE

Barbara Whitehead was born in Sheffield and has always lived in Yorkshire. She is currently the owner of the Brontë Birthplace in Thornton and resident there. She is a novelist and is working on a series of crime novels set in York, of which eight have been published so far. She has also written period novels and the non-fiction *Charlotte Brontë and her 'Dearest Nell', the story of a friendship.* Barbara is well known as a lecturer in Adult Education, mainly in family history and creative writing. She has three adult sons.

4. SORCERER'S APPRENTICE: PHARMACY IN PREWAR SHIPLEY

Alex Robinson was born in Esholt and educated at Esholt C of E School and Salt Boys' High School, Shipley. After apprenticeship to W.Rimmington Ltd, Shipley, he qualified as a pharmacist (MPS) from Bradford Technical College in 1937. He then managed a shop in Idle until 1940 when he rejoined Rimmingtons as a pharmacist. From 1943 to '46 he saw war service in the Army Intelligence Corps, and in 1949 he acquired his own pharmacy in Leeds. This closed in 1978. Since then he has been a locum pharmacist, chiefly with the Thorpe Green Pharmacy, Idle. Alex has lived in Idle since the war, having married an Idle girl in 1943. He has been treasurer of the Idle Musical Union, chairman of the Idle and Thackley Retired Men's Forum, and of the Idle and Thackley Heritage Group.

5. ON THE WAY TO THE TOP: JOHN BRAINE'S BRADFORD

Philip Colehan was a lifelong friend of John Braine. They met at Thackley School and then went together to St Bede's Grammar School. They both took up librarianship as a career and Philip worked in public libraries in Shipley, Sheffield, and Tottenham, before becoming the founder Borough Librarian of Hillingdon. Now retired, Philip lives with his wife in Uxbridge, Middlesex. John Braine called Philip 'the brother that I never had' and dedicated one of his books *The Pius Agent* to Philip and his wife Doreen.

6. BURNED TO THE GROUND: FIRES IN BRADFORD'S HISTORY

David Croft was born in Bradford and educated at Belle Vue Grammar School. He joined the staff of Bradford Libraries on leaving school and has worked in a number of the city's libraries, most notably as Local Studies Librarian from 1975 to 1985. He is now Assistant Area Librarian for the East Bradford Area. He studied librarianship at the Liverpool College of Commerce and was elected a Fellow of the Library Association in 1985. A life-long rail and road transport enthusiast, he has written a number of books on local transport and is currently researching the history of early Yorkshire bus operators. Other interests include walking and the history of seaside resorts.

7. FROM PARCEL LAD TO LEYLANDS: TROLLEYBUS TALES

Frank Long left school to become a parcels lad, conductor and trolleybus driver for Bradford Corporation. He left in 1953 after twenty four years (less war service) to work for Thompson and Pearson ('tea and pee') delivering soft drinks door to door in South Yorkshire. Promoted supervisor, manager, then Area Manager for their North East Region, he moved to Birmingham on becoming Company Sales Director for what was now Alpine Soft Drinks. On retirement, Frank moved back to Bradford where, with his wife of 51 years, he is a voluntary worker for the Bradford Talking Telegraph sending out tapes to the blind.

8. THE FLYING BOATS OF BRADFORD

Erik Blakeley began his higher education at Birmingham University by reading a B.Eng. and a PhD in metallurgy. After a PGCE at Leicester University and a two year sojourn teaching in Dorset, he returned to studies at the Institute of Archaeology, UCL, where he achieved an M.Sc in archaeometallurgy. A one year contract with the Royal Armouries in Leeds preceded his work for this article with the Bradford Industrial Museum. He is now working in Cumbria for an educational publisher.

Kevin Cairns came to Bradford in 1963 from Bangor, County Down. He served in the Royal Navy from 1964 until 1973. After leaving as a Leading Marine Engineering Mechanic he re-trained as a mechanical engineering draughtsman and worked in several engineering manufacturing companies in West Yorkshire. After redundancy and a short spell at sea in 1981, Kevin studied for a shipping and naval architecture degree at the Institute of Marine Studies in Plymouth. It was using this background that Kevin set out to catalogue and research the history of Bradford's naval aircraft blueprints.

Eugene Nicholson was educated at Margaret MacMillan School of Education. After a brief period in the Civil Service and Yorkshire Water, he studied part-time at Bradford University where he graduated in psychology. In 1988 he was appointed as Education Officer, and later, Assistant Keeper at the Bradford Industrial Museum. He became Senior Keeper of Technology in 1996. The cataloguing, research and publication on the history of Bradford's involvement in aircraft construction forms part of a process to gather together a definitive collection of objects for permanent display.

9. BRADFORD ITALIANS

Frederick Taglione was born into Bradford's Italian community in the late 1920s and educated at St Mary's Roman Catholic School, East Parade. He volunteered for the British Army at the age of sixteen and became a physical training instructor in the Green Howards. He was posted to Hanover and Berlin, where he met his future wife. He has been variously a painter, decorator, weaver, car sprayer and manager of a mini market freezer centre. On retirement, Fred started writing stories and now, at the age of seventy, is on his fifth book.

10. KEIGHLEY PRIDE

John Waddington-Feather was born in Keighley and educated at Keighley Boys' Grammar School and Leeds University. During National Service he was commissioned into the Army Intelligence Corps and gained his 'wings' as a paratrooper. He studied medicine for a while before making a career in teaching. John was ordained a priest in the Anglican Church in 1978 and is Assistant Prison Chaplain at Shrewsbury Gaol. John has been secretary of the Yorkshire Dialect Society and is founder Chairman of the J.B.Priestley Society. His publications include *Leeds:the heart of Yorkshire,* a history of Salts Grammar School, (where he once taught) and many volumes of poetry. John runs his own publishing house, Feather Books, and his verse play, *Garlic Street,* based on Keighley's Lawkholme Lane, recently enjoyed a successful run at Bingley's Little Theatre, and won a national award, The Burton Prize.

11. SALTAIRE: VISION TO VISION

 **Clive Woods** is a secondhand bookseller and local historian. Over the last twenty five years he has been actively promoting Saltaire and was a founder member of the Saltaire Village Society. At present, he is engaged in creating a Saltaire Archive and hopes, in the future, to create a Saltaire study centre and museum.

12. FAVOURITE HAUNTS AND HIDDEN CORNERS

Richard Newman was born and grew up in Bradford and presently lives in Eccleshill. For a number of years he worked in local government, then a Countryside Warden, and later as Education Liaison Officer in a Bradford upper school. He has also spent time working for Bradford Art Galleries and Museums. Richard is an active member of the management committee for the Undercliffe Cemetery Charity. He has always had an interest in local history, architecture, art, and photography. He is probably best known for his black and white photographs of local characters and eccentrics, exhibiting new work in the city centre each year for the Bradford Festival.

SUBJECT INDEX

PEOPLE INDEX

2)

Old Fallin, Cowie and Plean

Guthrie Hutton

THE ALLOA COAL Cº Section

Sᵗ Andrews Ambulance Corps.

COWIE.

© Guthrie Hutton, 2009
First published in the United Kingdom, 2009,
by Stenlake Publishing Ltd.
www.stenlake.co.uk
ISBN 978-1-84033-444-9

The building of Polmaise House, on the carselands close to the Forth, appears to have been started by John Murray in the 1690s. Subsequently altered, it remained the principal family home until 1866 when Polmaise Castle was built near Cambusbarron. By calling their new castle Polmaise, at some distance from the name's origins, the Murrays created no end of confusion!

ACKNOWLEDGEMENTS

Many of the pictures and much of the reference material for this book came from the collection amassed by the late Bob McCutcheon, one time book dealer of Spittal Street, Stirling. I am consequently very grateful to his widow Barbara for allowing me access to the material. I am also grateful to the staff at Stirling Library who helped to provide a lot of additional research and also the staff at the National Map Library, and the Royal Commission for the Ancient and Historical Monuments of Scotland, who filled in some of the gaps. I must also thank Dick Clarke for allowing me to use the picture of the Cowie Juveniles and the Scottish Mining Museum for the picture of Plean Colliery. I should also thank the many former miners who, over the years, have helped with my research into their industry.

FURTHER READING

Gifford, John, and Walker, Frank Arniel, *The Buildings of Scotland: Stirling and Central Scotland*, 2002.
Kerr, Hugh G., *Fallin: Tales from a Mining Village*,1991.
Royal Commission on the Ancient and Historical Monuments of Scotland, *Inventory of the Ancient and Historical Monuments of Stirlingshire* 2 vols, 1963.
Stirling District Libraries, *Cowie, Fallin and Plean in Old Photographs*, 1990.

Also by Guthrie Hutton for Stenlake Publishing:
Mining: From Kirkintilloch to Clackmannan and Stirling to Slamannan, 2000.
Scotland's Black Diamonds, 2001.
Old Bannockburn, 2008.

INTRODUCTION

Scotland's progress towards becoming an industrial nation began on Boxing Day 1760 when the first blast furnace at the Carron Ironworks was started up. Gradually the focus switched to Lanarkshire, with its abundant reserves of coal and ironstone. First the blast furnaces of Coatbridge and Shotts and then the steel works of Motherwell and Glasgow drove industrial development through the nineteenth century, but by the 1890s the Lanarkshire coal reserves were declining. At the same time, demand for coal was increasing and to meet it coal companies sank new large pits in Fife and the Lothians. They also turned their attention to the east of Stirling, where coal workings had hitherto been relatively small scale, and where vast reserves lay untapped beneath the carse.

Before large-scale coal mining moved in, the area had been occupied by a variety of peoples. At West Plean, in the 1950s, archaeologists discovered the remains of one of the most important Iron Age homestead sites in the country. It had evidently been built and rebuilt a number of times and was possibly still being lived in when the Romans first landed on the British Isles. These invaders later passed through the area, building a road for their armies to march from fort to fort as they sought to establish a presence in the country before pulling back to the Antonine Wall in 142 A.D.

Stirling's strategic position as the most easterly crossing of the Forth Estuary ensured that many more armies followed the Romans, tramping through the area to shape Scotland's turbulent history. Battles at Stirling, Falkirk and most famously Bannockburn show that this part of the country was on the fringe of some big events. In the long passages of time between such occasions local people got on with their lives, living in scattered communities and eking out a living in largely rural pursuits. Great estates and big houses also became part of the landscape.

The first large-scale industry was quarrying as the country's developing towns and cities used local stone for some of their buildings. Plean stone in particular was in demand. That industry was starting to falter at the end of the nineteenth century when big coal moved in. First, an invader from the north, the Alloa Coal Company sank a huge new pit and built the village of Cowie to house the miners. Then a Lanarkshire entrepreneur moved into Plean and while he was expanding the pit there a company from the Hamilton area sank two huge collieries to the east of Stirling. The second of these created the village of Fallin which, in four years, went from virtually nothing to a thriving community with a school and a church. Like the companies they worked for many of the mining families also came from the fading Lanarkshire industry.

The big collieries prospered for about sixty years, but Millhall closed in the 1950s with Plean and Bannockburn following in the 1960s. Fallin, which had acquired a reputation for industrial unrest, survived through the last great strike in 1984/85 before it too was closed.

The three villages have all erected memorials to the men who lost their lives in pursuit of coal and a larger display of mining artefacts has been set up at Fallin. Tiles and timber products have given Cowie another lease of industrial life while commuter housing is starting to change the area again. The physical impact of mining is fading, but memories linger and although the industry dominated the area for less than 100 years it will always be a big part of its story.

Early twentieth century miners on the cage at Bannockburn Colliery, Cowie, with an iron bar providing only the most rudimentary protection.

Steuarthall, also known as Wester Polmaise, was a delightful Scots vernacular house situated in a crook of the Bannock Burn near Old Polmaise House. Although some elements of the building reflected a style prevalent in the 17th or even 16th centuries the house is thought to have been built about 1700 for Archibald Stirling of Garden following his marriage to Anna, daughter of Sir Alexander Hamilton of Haggs. The kitchen arrangements were updated in 1824 when the main wing of the house was extended to the rear. The building was clearly still occupied when this early 20th century picture was taken. It was described in the early 1960s as having fallen into disrepair and being used in the previous decade 'for poultry'.

Fallin, described in the mid nineteenth century as 'a small harbour on the river Forth at which coals and lime are shipped', was transformed when Archibald Russell Ltd. started sinking two shafts in August 1904. Although the company's founder hailed from Clackmannanshire his career as a coal master began in 1843 at Cambuslang, near Glasgow. He established a family business which later developed pits in the Hamilton area before turning its attention to Stirlingshire. The new shafts were driven through soft alluvial deposits, something the industry had not been able to do before. They reached a variety of seams. There was anthracite, a coal which burned hot and smokeless; navigation coal, for ships; coking coal, which was needed by the iron and steel industry; and ordinary household coal. The colliery, named Polmaise Nos. 3 and 4, went into production in April 1906.

Polmaise Nos. 1 and 2 had been sunk by Archibald Russell Ltd. two years earlier at a site approximately midway between Fallin and Stirling town centre. Despite its official Polmaise title this colliery was better known as Millhall. It could also boast of having a large briquetting plant where soft dross coal was bound with pitch into blocks of combustible fuel; different shapes and sizes were made for industrial and domestic purposes. The pits at Millhall and Fallin worked independently of each other until the workings converged in 1931 and a connection was made between them. Although the senior pit by a couple of years Millhall closed earlier in June 1958.

Millhall

These bandsmen are wearing Gladstone collars and bow ties, a form of neckwear only ever worn by the Millhall Pipe Band, but just to confuse the historian someone has written Fallin Colliery on the back of the picture. The Millhall Band, set up in 1919 under Pipe Major George D. McDonald, gained a place in piping history when it won the Argyll Shield, a trophy regarded as the world championship, in 1924. They won it again in 1926 and in 1930, but Pipe Major McDonald left the band after that to take up a full-time post with the army and the Millhall Band quickly fell apart. Fallin's pipe band appears to have acted as a feeder to Millhall during its years of success, but outlasted it, continuing in existence through to the 1950s.

Two-storey brick-built blocks known, unsurprisingly, as The Blocks were built for the miners. A newspaper report, which indicated that construction was due to commence in April 1906, also gave an indication of the thinking that lay behind such provision. It speculated that the 180 houses could accommodate about 800 people because, allowing for the miner, his family and their lodger or lodgers, each dwelling could hold six people - 'which is not too big an average for a miner's dwelling'. These words suggest an attitude that placed miners in a separate social structure because the houses were at best a room and kitchen or 'single ends' (as dwellings of only one room were known).

Fallin

The blocks were supplied with running water for domestic use and pit water for flushing toilets which were shared between two houses. Despite this concession to better standards the blocks were not well built and soon suffered from damp and infestations of wood lice, beetles and other insects. The unpaved ground quickly turned to mud when wet and dust when dry - there was no escape from dirt. Faced with such difficulties and no realistic alternative the residents created a self-reliant society in which neighbours looked out for each other. They also lived in a kind of communal harmony, born of hardship that has disappeared from today's consumer-driven society. The blocks were demolished in the 1950s.

The housing built for the miners and their families at Fallin was necessary because the pit was too far away from established centres like Stirling or Bannockburn for all the miners to live there. Also, the hundreds of families moving into the area to work at the new collieries would otherwise have placed a massive burden on the existing infrastructure. The company decided, however, that Millhall was sufficiently close to the existing towns that there was no need to provide housing for its miners, although they did build thirty cottages at the colliery entrance for officials. There were twenty similar houses built for officials at Fallin which are seen here with the colliery gates in the background.

Fallin

Pit villages, built to serve one large colliery, were often in thrall to the mining company which could more or less control anything that happened in the village. They could, and often did, successfully stop anyone opening a pub which they regarded as likely to lead to social ills and drunkenness at work. The Industrial and Providential Societies Act of 1893, however, allowed co-operative pubs to be set up where profits from the sale of drink could be ploughed back into community ventures. It was based on a Swedish idea and so such pubs were known as Gothenburgs or 'Goths'. The one at Fallin, opened in 1910, is seen here in 1928 with, in the background, the miners' welfare hall which was completed in 1924.

The Goth was very much at the heart of the village, directly across the road from the blocks. The bar was on the ground floor, while upstairs there were meeting and function rooms, and a library. A separate stair meant that women and children could go to these without having to encounter the demon drink. Management of the Goth was disinterested in that there was no incentive to sell more drink to enhance profits, but there was a payoff for the customers who knew that they were helping to improve the village. There was also a benefit to the mining company who could cheerfully wait for the Goth to come up with the money for things they might otherwise have had to fund themselves. One facility made possible by the Goth was the bowling green, laid out beside the building's gable end.

Opposite: The Bowling Green was completed in April 1911 when Mrs Murray of Polmaise laid the final piece of turf. Two months later, on 3 June the official opening was performed by R. S. Horne K.C. - that'll be him in the upper picture addressing the throng squeezed onto the narrow verge between the building and the green. In the lower picture a wee boy provides a sharp contrast, standing barefooted amongst the better shod and besuited adults. The new clubhouse, paid for by the Goth, was opened in June 1912. The green proved to be an important and popular element of village life, hosting local and district competitions. Members of the Polmaise Club have also taken part in County and Scottish competitions.

This view looking west towards Stirling shows Main Street running through Fallin with four of the blocks in the background and the school on the left. A little school on the same site had served the scattered rural community before the colliery was opened, but as Fallin grew and the blocks filled up the need to provide a new, larger primary school became increasingly urgent. It was a race against time for the St Ninian's School Board through the first half of 1907 with each new classroom being occupied as soon as it was completed. In early May there were 122 pupils, eight more were expected within a week, 35 would be coming by the middle of the month and the roll was expected to reach 210 by mid-June. The hastily erected school was replaced by a new one 60 years later.

There was much flag waving and patriotism on show at Fallin's Peace Day in August 1919. The village children are assembled here in front of the school with, on the right, a youthful pipe band. They and their somewhat older kilted leader, Drum Major McNeill, are perhaps symbolic of the war's lost generation of young men. After listening to a short address, and singing a psalm and the National Anthem, the children lined up behind the pipers to march through the village to the Recreation Park where games and a picnic were laid on. There were sports, quoiting and five-a-side football for adults too. On the wall behind the pipers in this picture is a lovely detail of early twentieth century school life; the bell which would have been rung to summon the children to their lessons.

While the Goth catered for the earthly needs of Fallin folk their spiritual needs - at least those who worshipped as Protestants - were met by the new church, erected at the eastern end of the village. It can be seen on the right hand edge of this early twentieth century picture which also shows Main Street reverting to a roughly defined country road as soon as it leaves the village. The church was designed by Stirling architects McLuckie and Walker and built of Polmaise stone, not brick as was originally intended. It was paid for with contributions from well-wishers including Archibald Russell Ltd., but the principal benefactor was James Murray of Polmaise who also granted use of the site on favourable terms. He was present at the laying of the foundation stone in 1907, but had died before the first sermon was preached in September 1908 by the Rt. Rev'd. Dr. Theodore Marshall, the Moderator of the Church of Scotland.

Fallin

The church is seen to better advantage in this view from 1928 which also shows the addition of a bellcote to the street-facing gable, which has since been removed. In front of the church is the war memorial. This simple obelisk was unveiled in November 1919, making it one of the first in Scotland. It commemorated the men of Fallin, Throsk, Millhall and Loanhead, who had died fighting in the First World War. After a short service in the church the congregation moved outside to watch Major A. B. Murray of Polmaise unveil the monument. This was followed by more speeches and suitable music from the Fallin Pipe Band and the Salvation Army Band. The ceremony was completed by a bugler from the Argyll & Sutherland Highlanders playing the last post. Two weeks later the village held a supper dance to welcome home the men who had survived the war.

The pictures on these two pages show the houses of West and East Throsk in 1928 shortly after they were built on either side of the access road to the Bandeath Royal Naval Armaments Depot (RNAD). With the exception of the removal of some chimney heads, altered windows and addition of satellite television dishes, little has changed. The RNAD was set up during the First World War, supplanting a brick and tile works which had operated in the area from the early part of the nineteenth century up to 1916. When the armaments depot closed in the late 1970s it covered a 700 acre site which was taken over by Central Regional Council and converted into the Bandeath Industrial Estate.

The brick and tile works which preceded the RNAD was the last element of a pottery industry which had thrived in the vicinity of Throsk throughout the seventeenth and early eighteenth centuries. The Throsk potters, or piggers as they were sometimes known, made a wide variety of practical wares including storage jars, jugs, bowls and 'pigs', narrow-necked pots used to contain liquids or, sometimes, money - piggy banks! They used clay dug from pits in the carselands and possibly fired the pots with local coal, or perhaps wood or peat from the Bandeath Peninsula. It is possible that for a time Throsk could have accounted for the largest concentration of potters in the country. Boats working up or down the Forth would have taken their wares to all the major markets.

Bannockburn Colliery, the first industrial-scale pit to the east of Stirling, was developed by the Alloa Coal Company who were operating outside their Clackmannanshire base for the first time. Work began in March 1893 and it took two years for the two rectangular shafts, set 25 yards apart, to reach the valuable Bannockburn Main seam at a depth of just over 1,000 feet. The Main, along with the Hartley seam, produced a high quality coking coal. The pithead, with the winding engine house on the left, the wooden headframes, centre, and the large preparation plant on the right was a classic state of the art colliery layout for the later nineteenth and early twentieth centuries.

Some of the coal produced at the pit was burned on the premises. These men are thought to have been responsible for keeping the boilers fired to produce the steam needed to power the various installations at the pit. These included the winding engine and a pumping engine which had to keep the constant problem of water ingress under control. The pit was expanded in 1902/03 when a third shaft was sunk at the appropriately named Sink Farm. The colliery was taken over in 1936 by the Carron Company and closed in 1953 although a drift mine, opened to the Upper Hirst seam in the same year, kept mining going until 1964.

To house their workers the Alloa Coal Company created the pit village of Cowie, described in an old poem as '*A dirty, dreary, dismal hole; Whaur folk exist by diggin coal*', and where '*The raws are built wi' hauf fired brick; The roads wi' muck are three feet thick*'. These vivid words say more about the village than much of the heartfelt language often used to describe miners' rows. The poet's 'hauf fired bricks' are a perfect description of cheap construction, crumbling materials and damp. Also, the 'muck' that the roads were made of could be a mixture of almost anything: mud, ashes, coal dust and sundry other unmentionable ingredients. Superb! The picture shows McGowan Row.

Cowie

As with any walk of life the coal industry had its hierarchy with seniority being rewarded with more money and, in the company villages, better housing. Rows like Murray Row, with its evidently superior houses, will have been allocated to oversmen, tradesmen etc. It was named after the Murrays of Polmaise who leased the mineral rights to the company. These houses have gardens and the tenants have fulfilled the company's expectation, and used them to grow fruit and vegetables; it looks like a model village and contrasts somewhat with the bleak little poem quoted on the previous page.

The Bannockburn Co-operative Society opened its branch at Cowie in March 1904. Prior to that the village had been served by the Society's vans and so, when the shops opened, there were already 160 Co-op members in Cowie. The Society was one of the oldest in the country, having been formed in 1830. To begin with it was structured like a joint stock company with members receiving bonus payments based on their shareholding. This structure differed from the system of paying dividends on purchases, as used by the Rochdale Equitable Pioneers Society which is widely regarded as the model from which the co-operative movement grew. Co-operators generally preferred the Rochdale system and so the Bannockburn Society switched to it in 1865. In 1906 the Society also opened a branch at Plean, where it operated in competition with the Falkirk Society.

This picture shows the shops to the right of the Co-op on the facing page. It was probably taken a year or two after 1907 when the two-storey building on the right was completed. The ground floor shops were initially occupied by a Mr. Marsh from Falkirk who ran a fish restaurant and Miss McLauchlan, a local woman, who opened a drapery and millinery. In the adjacent building Mr. Haliburton, who ran a newsagent's business and hairdresser's, took over the Post Office in 1904. The Co-op will no doubt have given these small shops stiff competition, especially The Dividend Stores in the single-storey building. These shop buildings in Main Street, and those of the Co-op, have outlasted the rows, perhaps because they were built of stone, a more substantial material than the poet's 'hauf-fired' bricks.

The church in Cowie also came in for some caustic comment from our poet:

There is a kirk - there's only yin,
On Sunday it is aye hauf tim (empty),
Auld Nick's nae need tae look for sin,
'gin he just comes tae Cowie.

Initially church services in Cowie were held in the village hall which had been provided by the Alloa Coal Company. Things improved in 1905 when a United Free Church was built in the village and this in turn became part of the Church of Scotland when the churches reunited in 1929. While these arrangements served the spiritual needs of the Protestant population, Roman Catholics had to wait a little longer. Many of the families coming to live in the mining villages had moved from

Lanarkshire, bringing their religion with them, and Cowie became the centre for Roman Catholic worship for the surrounding area. The parish was established in 1898, but the original church was superseded by the Church of the Sacred Heart, erected to the designs of architect Reginald Fairlie in 1937. At this time the parish was split, with Cowie and Fallin forming a separate parish to Bannockburn and Plean. The stylish brick-built structure sits on an eminence with fine views of Stirling Castle and over the Forth to the Ochil Hills and the Wallace Monument.

Football was enjoyed by mining communities whose teams often achieved success, as the Cowie Juveniles did when they won through to the final of the Scottish Juvenile Cup in June 1929. The game was played at Shawfield Park, Glasgow, and their opponents, Park United, came from the Kinning Park area of the city. The Cowie team were not without supporters, because a special train from Plean Station brought 500 from the village to cheer them on. They could also hear the familiar strains of the Bannockburn Colliery Band, one of three bands which entertained the crowd before the game. Cowie won by four goals to two. Football was also a good way out of the pits for many young men and John McPhee, who played on the right wing in the game, was signed later by Sunderland.

Band music was popular in mining communities and a source of pride for those involved. The bands were paid for either by fund-raising in the community or through weekly contributions from the men at the pit. The Bannockburn Colliery Band appears to have been formed early in 1903 and in May of that year paraded with its new instruments through the streets of Bannockburn. Mr Hastie of Cambusbarron, the conductor, was praised on that occasion for having got the band to such a high standard in so short a time. The bandsmen's efforts were certainly rewarded after their performance when, on the invitation of Mr. Nisbet, they adjourned to his Klondyke Bar for some refreshment. The naval style of uniform was adopted in 1928, something of a change from the military look of the band's first uniforms.

Cowie District and Polmaise Pipe Band was formed in March 1905 with a large number of players hoping to become bandsmen under the direction of Mr. Dickson Christie. In early June, with less than three months' practice behind them, they turned out at Plean Sports for their first public performance. Two weeks later, the band was back at Plean for a continuation of the sports and when they had finished playing there they went on to Bannockburn to parade along the principal streets. Before their long day was over they returned to Cowie and marched up and down the rows, to the delight of the local people. The band is seen here in front of the bowling green clubhouse in a picture used as a postcard in 1912. The bowling green was laid in 1908.

The Alloa Coal Company expanded their operations in Stirlingshire in 1903 when they started to sink a new pit at Carnock, to the east of Bannockburn Colliery. Initially the work was delayed by the time it took to extend the railway, but the colliery was producing high quality coking coal by 1908. Coke ovens were set up to extract gases and other impurities which were then turned into tar, sulphate of ammonia and other by-products in an adjacent plant. The coke was vital for iron smelting and the nearby Carron Company, which had come to depend on Carnock's output, secured the plant for themselves when they bought all of the Alloa Coal Company's Stirlingshire operations in 1936.

Carnock House, or Castle, once one of the grandest houses in Scotland, was built about 1548 by Robert Drummond. He later became Master of Works to the Scottish Crown and his interest in design and construction probably accounted for the splendour of the building. In 1634 the Carnock estates passed to Thomas Nicholson who appears to have set about altering and adding to the structure almost immediately because a stone bearing that date was set into the south wall. The house later passed to the Shaw family of Greenock who made only minor alterations, so the building, complete with ornamental plaster work and painted decoration would have been a gem of historical Scottish building and design had it not been demolished in 1941. The inset picture (below) shows a lodge at the castle gate.

The drill hall beside Cowie Loan survived the mining era, although not as a military establishment. It is seen here a few years before the outbreak of the First World War. Going to war was a more exciting prospect than working underground and by 1916 so many miners had joined the forces that low output levels were threatening the war effort. In an effort to keep men in the pits, the government stopped them from joining up and also started to repatriate miners from the front. Astonishingly the same thing happened in the Second World War with protected status not being given to the industry until 1941. By 1943 the situation was so serious that one in ten young men were conscripted into the mines instead of the forces. They were known as Bevin Boys after Ernest Bevin, the minister of Labour who introduced the measure.

Cowie

Sceptics scoffed at the proposal to build the Scottish Central Railway which was authorised in 1845 to run from a field near Bonnybridge to Perth - on the face of it a line from nowhere to what was then a minor destination. It was opened to Stirling in March 1848 and Perth a couple of months later. As soon as it was completed connections were made with the Edinburgh and Glasgow railway and tracks coming up from England, making the line an essential link in the country's growing railway network. It was taken over by the Caledonian Railway in the 1860s and was still being operated by them when the big Stirlingshire pits were developed. To some extent the siting of a pithead was determined by the ease with which tracks could be laid into it and so the planners of the Polmaise, Bannockburn and Plean Collieries must have blessed those early pioneers who laid the Scottish Central. The upper picture, which looks south to Plean Station, shows the tracks joining from Bannockburn Colliery on the left and on the right the branch line leading toward Plean Colliery. The lower picture shows Plean Station, which was opened in 1904 to cater for the passenger traffic generated by the pit villages. It closed in 1956.

Francis Simpson made his fortune, first as a soldier and then as commander of a merchant vessel trading in the far east. He returned to Scotland about 1800, acquired Plean Estate and carried out various improvements including the building of Plean House. It was acquired in 1894 by Wallace Thorneycroft whose family had been in the coal business in Lanarkshire for three previous generations. With pits almost surrounding the house and working the minerals under it, few coal owners can have lived quite so close to the 'shop' as Wallace Thorneycroft. When he retired in 1929 he and his wife moved to Devon. The house remained in the family, but became a ruin after it was abandoned in 1970 and the contents sold. Plean Country Park was established in the grounds in 1993.

Plean was an established colliery when Wallace Thorneycroft acquired it and set up the Plean Colliery Company to work the coal reserves on the estate. He was the company's managing director, but also an accomplished mining engineer who instigated a development plan which included the sinking of a new shaft, No. 4. It was completed in 1901 and worked the same seams as the neighbouring pits, producing a high quality coking coal which was processed at the pit's own coke ovens. That the Bannockburn Main coal was volatile was cruelly demonstrated in July 1922 when an explosion in the Carbrook section of the pit killed twelve men and injured seven. It was the worst loss of life in a single incident in any of the large Stirlingshire pits. The cause was an improperly stemmed shot, but the company was blamed for not having applied sufficient stone dust, as required by law, to suppress the coal dust and reduce the severity of an explosion.

Before Wallace Thorneycroft took over at Plean, some of the miners' housing there was poorly made and even compared badly to Fallin's blocks and Cowie's rows. Stirling County Council was so appalled by a report delivered by their sanitary inspectors in the early 1890s that they were prepared to condemn the buildings before they were occupied. Earth was piled against the walls making the interiors so damp that the inspectors regarded the houses as uninhabitable and they would only consider them as fit for occupation when the earth had been excavated, the interior walls lathed and plastered, and timber floors put in with ventilation underneath. The later housing built for the Plean Colliery Company was better, although not good. This view, looking west along Main Street, shows the houses which were made of red brick and known collectively as the Red Rows. In the distance is Plean Tavern and the little shop which faces the camera on the next page.

Some of the Red Rows can be seen on the left of this view looking up what is now President Kennedy Drive to Cadger's Loan. The loan crossed the Roman Road a mile from where this picture was taken. At the intersection of the two roads was Plean No. 3 pit and a miners' row associated with it, Bore Row, ran alongside the Roman Road. It drew scathing comment from the county's sanitary inspector. In his report he described an absence of proper toilet accommodation and how waste was disposed of in open drains - sheughs - set at about twelve feet from the front doors of the houses. These were fed under the road and allowed to discharge into a field. In a corner of the same field was a hole close to a burn from which people were expected to draw their water, but it was subject to both weather conditions and contamination by the sewage from the drainage channel.

This view, taken about 1910, looks down from Cadger's Loan with the rows on the right and the football pitch on the left in front of Plean Hall. The hall, opened in January 1909, had space to seat 500 people and there was also a billiard room with two tables.

When the coal industry was nationalised in 1947 the miners' housing became the property of the new National Coal Board. They entered into discussions with Stirling County Council to rehouse the tenants and demolish the old buildings. The council devised a scheme in 1950 to encourage the residents to move to nearby places like Larbert or Bannockburn and issued forms to find out where people would like to move to. Some agreed to go elsewhere, to Prestwick in one case, but the majority of people expressed a desire to remain in Plean.

Plean Hall was paid for by contributions of a penny a week deducted from miners' wages, as well as contributions from the company, and in that respect it foreshadowed the miners' welfare fund, set up under the Mining Industry Act of 1920. That fund was also made up of contributions of a penny a week deducted from the miners' pay, plus a penny levied on every ton of coal. The money had to be spent in the areas where it was raised and it was left to local committees, made up of representatives from the management and the men, to decide what they wanted. In Plean the existing hall was extended at the rear to include six bathrooms for miners and their families, a lesser hall, or committee room, and a caretaker's house. The improved facility was opened in September 1924 by Mrs Wallace Thorneycroft. The welfare scheme was extended in 1926 to provide funds for pithead baths.

There seems always to have been a cluster of shops at the west end of Main Street, as this view looking toward Bannockburn in the 1920s shows. The village post office, once a hub of village life, can be seen with its sign advertising a public telephone. The sign has gone, but most of these buildings have survived to the present day although the hut on the right, where the boot and shoe repairer sits with his dog at an open door, is no longer there. In the background is the embankment carrying the colliery railway to the bridge over the main road. Now a new embankment and bridge carries the M9 motorway over the main road at the same spot; sometimes the more things change the more they stay the same.

Plean

This view shows the village from the colliery railway line, with the buildings shown on the facing page now seen on the left. The empty ground to the left and right has since been taken up with the housing of Burnside Crescent and Loanfoot Gardens built by Stirling County Council. In 1919 parliament gave local authorities powers to erect social housing for rent. The legislation was enacted in response to the report of a Royal Commission, set up in 1912, to look into housing provision. Its shocking conclusions brought about a fundamental change in the way society provided housing and the first Parliamentary Act was followed by others extending the authorities' powers.

Council housing like Loanfoot Gardens to some extent met the aspiration that grew during the First World War to provide homes 'fit for heroes' and so it makes a fitting backdrop to the war memorial. It was unveiled by General Sir Charles Monro, Bart. on 6 August 1922, less than a month after the explosion at Plean Colliery had claimed the lives of more men from the village. The ceremonial was accompanied by music from Plean Silver Band and the Millhall Pipe Band. Plean also had cause to remember one soldier from the village who was not killed, Sergeant John McAulay V.C. of the 1st Scots Guards. During an attack to the west of Cambrai, in November 1917, the 2nd Guards Brigade came under heavy machine gun fire. Sergeant McAulay's officer was fatally wounded, but he carried him to a dugout 400 yards away and then returned to the attack, killing about 50 of the enemy with a Lewis gun. His heroism earned him a Victoria Cross, but the Guards' action failed.

There are a lot of children in the pictures of miners' housing in this book. In those days large families were commonplace and the rapid growth of the mining industry and its associated villages created a problem for the education authorities. They were required by the Education Act of 1872 to provide schooling for all children between the ages of five and thirteen, but while this was previously done in small buildings, quite suddenly more accommodation was needed. At Plean, where the schoolhouse dates from 1874, the St. Ninian's School Board engaged Mr. Walker, of Stirling architects McLuckie and Walker, to draw up plans for an enlarged building in 1902. They also sought advice from Wallace Thorneycroft as to when any new housing would be built and occupied. Armed with this information they went ahead and completed the new school building in 1904.

William Simpson's Home was established by Colonel Francis Simpson of Plean House in memory of his son William, a sickly young man who had died just before his 22nd birthday in 1827. It was opened in 1836 as an asylum, a place of peace and solitude, 'for the reception, residence, and entertainment of indigent or reduced men of advanced age who may have served in the navy or army'. Although this latter distinction was not a binding condition of admittance, the home did acquire an unofficial title of the 'sailor's home'. The building was constructed using local Plean stone to the designs of Dunblane architect William Stirling and enlarged in 1872.

The home is still in existence providing care for old men as it always did. It sits amidst farmland on the north side of the main A9 road surrounded by six acres of garden grounds. Within the gardens is this fine villa known as Pleanholm which also serves as part of the home. Its roof line has been altered with the addition of dormer windows which had been installed by the 1950s. At that time the rules were strict, although the old soldiers and sailors may have appreciated an ordered life in which they had to be clean and tidy at all times. Prayers were an important part of the regime and a section of the Plean Parish Church was set aside for them for worship. The trustees of the William Simpson Estate had also contributed ground and provided the funds for the building of the church.

Inside, the home was well-appointed, as these pictures from the 1950s show. At that time there were 20 bedrooms for 42 men, so they had to share sleeping accommodation. They also had the use of two lounges, a library and a large dining hall. Meals, prepared in the well-equipped kitchen, were served at set times. There was a nursing sister on staff and an on-call doctor who visited the home every two weeks. Clothes were laundered on site and there were free visits from a barber and chiropodist. The men were not allowed to leave the premises outside set hours without permission and their visitors also had to adhere to strict visiting times. Drink, other than that required for medicinal purposes, was prohibited.

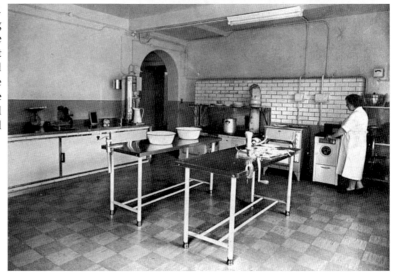

This view looking east through the old village of Plean has changed in a number of ways. The house jutting into the picture on the left has gone, as has the little cottage beyond it. These have been replaced by more modern housing, but perhaps the most striking change is in the methods used to carry wires and cables. Telegraph poles, seen here on the right, used to be everywhere, lining the edges of roads and railway lines, and marching over fields, but now they have largely disappeared, the wires they carried having been replaced by fibre-optic cables buried in underground pipes. Meanwhile, if this picture was taken today, the view would include a large, if distant, electricity pylon. Perhaps it too will be replaced by a less obtrusive technology one day!

These cottages on Cardrowan Road present a fine contrast to the miner's rows of the nearby villages. Although somewhat altered they are still there, unlike the more transient structures erected for the coal industry - not that they were far from a major installation, Plean No. 5 shaft, which was sunk on the other side of the main road in 1931. It must have come as a rude shock to the occupants of the houses whose pleasant view of a field was replaced by one of a noisy, smoky, dirty pithead. The new shaft was needed because the underground workings extended so far from the base of No. 4 that haulage distances were becoming impractical. The two pits were linked on the surface by a mineral railway (more smoke) which ran alongside the main road and through Plean Estate. The colliery closed in 1962.

Old Plean